Poking the Bear: A guide for engaging in the conversations that matter most.
Her way, his way, your way, their way.

Questions and answers to get the ball rolling in your school, department, PLC, and staff meeting

There are no taboo topics in education.

Dave Schmittou, Ed.D
and
Katelynn Giordano, MSEd

Dedications

Katelynn:
To every person who has felt quieted or unable to find the words, this book is first and foremost for you. In my life, professional and personal, I have had moments where I felt small and silenced. Like I had nothing to offer in a conversation, or that I could not possibly be enough to affect change. Finding the courage to stand up and speak out has become my passion because the change we want only happens when we work for it — all of us, together. Your words, your voice, your input, matter. We have the power and potential to move mountains. And to every one of you who has challenged me, pushed me, supported me, checked me, and helped me grow, I could not have done this without you.

Dave:
This book is dedicated to everyone who has walked into my life and helped me become the person I am today. Odds are, I am a different person today than when you knew me and that's why I am grateful. Today, every day, I continue to evolve. I am growing and I am changing. My beliefs and my thoughts shift daily. I am not flip-flopping. I am growing.
Your words, your thoughts, your actions have helped me refine who I am. You have helped chip away at the stone and soften the rough edges. Thank you for pushing me, for prodding me, for pulling me along, and for poking me.

Contents

Chapter 1

Waking from hibernation

Before you dive into this book with a highlighter in hand, seeking the silver bullet or magic pill to drive your students to academic mastery and creating amazing data, you should know that's not necessarily what you are going to get here (although we both believe that this book will lead to amazing growth). This is not a book that you are expected to read cover to cover in one sitting, starting with this introduction and finishing with the conclusion. This is a book designed to give you the freedom to bounce around, to pick and choose your topics, to allow for a variety of readers and learners to grapple with concepts of their own choosing and in their own order. You do not need to read Chapter 2: "Do as I did" to understand Chapter 9: "Does competition belong...." You can begin with Chapter 14: "Do kids need a dress code?" and later proceed to Chapter 6: "What is the purpose of a grade?" and still gain value. In fact, we believe you will gain more value in attacking this book in this format, as it will allow you to address what you need when you need it.

This book is also not a "how to" manual filled with prescriptive protocols that you just need to follow in three easy steps. This is a book intentionally designed with you in mind, because you and your colleagues are helping us write this book. That's right. You are an author of the book you are holding. As you dig in, you will see that we (Dave and Katelynn) have shared our thoughts, our Two Cents as we call them, simply to help get the conversations started. We acknowledge that there are often additional elements to the conversations that we have not addressed. We admit that we do not know your circumstances, your experiences, or your communities. We believe it is easier to steer a car that is already in motion, than to start a movement from a standstill so we share our opinions to help you shape and share yours. We hope to give you the momentum that you are free to use to move to a new direction. We encourage you to disagree, to debate, and to push back. We share what we believe to help you articulate what you believe. We know that sometimes it is easier for you to begin the needed conversations by debating what others have already said, so we share to provide that starting point, that space to begin the conversations.

But our voices should not be the voices that matter most. Your voice matters. The voices of your peers matter. We are just two educators willing to share and we encourage you to do the same.

We believe that there are no taboo topics in education. We believe that any conversation we are willing to have with students should be a conversation we are willing to have with our colleagues. We believe that if our school community really is a family, as we so often profess it to be, we need to be willing to have the difficult discussions, to debate the topics that matter most to us, to embrace the people we love and depend on, while questioning the ideas and practices that define what we do. We believe that asking questions, challenging beliefs, and impacting change will bring discomfort, but that in discomfort, we find growth. We believe that you can debate a concept, disagree with an approach, and push those around you, all the while maintaining a level of professional respect. We believe conversations lead to actions and actions lead to results. We believe that educators are amazing people with incredible insights. We believe we are better together and that we all have the ability to grow and learn. We believe we all have gifts to share, knowledge to deliver, and wisdom to contribute. We believe that conversations must be had so collective growth can happen. We believe that humility is the willingness to listen and learning is simply changing our minds. We believe this book will empower you to celebrate this, to accept this, and hopefully acquire innovative thoughts and practices that will not only benefit you as an educator and person, but your students as learners and leaders.

This book has been written with dozens of conversation starters. These questions are all things we have either been asked or been confronted with in our careers. As we discussed the topics in this book, they tended to fall into a few categories: purpose of education, grades, equity, student voice, teacher voice, professional growth, and change. Each time we broached these topics, we were reminded of a story or personal experience one or both of us had that shaped our opinion. So after each question you will be able to read the thoughts that each of us has on the topic. Before each question, you'll get a chance to hear some of these original stories. We attempted to keep our opinions out of these stories, but because many of them are true and personal for us, it was difficult at times to separate our perspectives from the narrative. Neither one of us are experts. The two of us are on our own journeys, and this book does not represent our endpoints. Rather, we're inviting you into this journey with us, and to continue your own personal evolution as an educator and person. So as you read, consider your own stories, related experiences, and the two very real, very flawed human beings behind this book.

Katelynn is a middle school teacher in Illinois, a wife, a cat mom, and a speaker/consultant. Dave is a professor of Educational Leadership, former school administrator, husband, father of four, and an author. After you have the chance to read our thoughts, there is a space for you to write your thoughts, called "A Penny for My Thoughts." This is an opportunity for you to articulate your beliefs, your understandings, and your perceptions, so that you are prepared to share them with others. Each section also includes an area for you to take notes on the thoughts of your peers — "A Penny for Their Thoughts." This is where you can capture their words, their ideas, and their insights. This is where your thinking can be solidified, molded, shaped, challenged, and grown. Our hope is that after each conversation, you will take the time to reflect on what you have learned and that you identify areas in which you hope to keep growing as well as questions you hope to be able to answer in the future. We are not attempting to change your point of view. As a matter of fact, we willingly admit that much of what we currently believe as we write this could be dramatically different by the time you choose to read this. We put our thoughts out there, not to convince, but to aid in the debate. As you begin your conversations, we encourage you to begin yours in much the same way we are beginning ours. Admit that you could be wrong. Express a desire to learn and grow. Challenge your own assumptions and question the assertions of others.

This book is the first spark to start a flame that has the potential to set your school and district on fire. But keep in mind, this book is only that first spark. It is up to you to cultivate and fan the flames that you nurture with the fuel you provide. We are here to help you start the conversations. We are here to simply Poke the Bear. It is up to you to roar, to grow, to learn, to wake from your hibernation, and make the magic happen. Lean into each other, respect each other, and challenge everything, especially what you think you know. Our "two cents" is small change compared to all that you and your team are capable of making sense of. So hold on tight, pick a topic, and let the poking begin.

Part One

The Purpose

[pur-puhs] the reason for which something exists or is done, made, used, etc.

— Dictionary.com

"It's the essence of our humanity—to create, to invent, to make our world better."

— Ted Dintersmith, What School Could Be: Insights and Inspiration from Teachers Across America

"With well-designed pedagogy, we can empower kids with critical skills and help them turn passions into decisive life advantages. The role of education is no longer to teach content, but to help our children learn—in a world that rewards the innovative and punishes the formulaic."

— Tony Wagner, Most Likely to Succeed: Preparing Our Kids for the Innovation Era

Learning happens in so many environments, both inside and outside of school. In its purest form, learning is simply a collection of memories. As we gain experience, our memories stack upon themselves allowing us to make predictions and inferences based upon our past. So much of what we know we have learned by simply living life. So what is the purpose of school if we can learn simply by living?

∾

Jackson loved being a Boy Scout. He looked forward every year to attending summer camp where he explored independence and collaboration. He was three hours from his house but felt at home. He learned to start a fire, to fish, to tie knots, to swim, to cook spaghetti, and how to put himself back to sleep at night when he woke up from a scary dream. He learned how to be confident and how to stay humble. He learned how to work hard and how to persist when faced with resistance. Looking back on it today, Jackson will happily tell you that Boy Scouts helped him learn how to be a successful man.

∾

Sharmaine was a baller. She woke up early every day during the summer so she could get to the local YMCA before everyone else. She wanted to make sure she had time to work on her free throws and her crossover dribble while the gym was still quiet. As others began to wake up and find their way to the basketball courts, Sharmaine was often the only girl in the game. Playing against others who hadn't put in the work that she did gave her an advantage, even if most were taller and stronger. She was fierce. Her commitment allowed her to earn a scholarship to attend a Division 1 school in the northeast where she eventually met the man who is now the father to her two daughters, each of whom is also fiercely independent and competitive. The oldest is now a star field hockey player on her high school team. The youngest is a kicker on the varsity football team— the only girl on the team.

~

Carlos loved his job as a member of the safety patrol. As a fifth grader, he had the opportunity to help walk the school's kindergarten students to the busses and then stand at the crosswalk assisting those students who were walking home. Prior to this year, Carlos was a shy child. He had a difficult time making friends and was often timid when called on by his teachers in class. Now, it was as if the bright orange safety patrol belt and badge that he wore gave him a new identity. What the cape was to Clark Kent, the polyester belt was to Carlos. A protector of the innocent. A defender of safety. Carlos was a safety patrol boy and the school community was better because of him.

~

Ms. Jasmin was the school's new seventh grade teacher. Fresh out of college, Ms. Jasmin was already becoming a favorite teacher of every 12-year-old lucky enough to have her listed on their schedule. During the school day, she helped every child feel seen. Before every class, she found herself standing at the door so she could greet each child as they entered and so she could wish good luck to every child on their way out. Before the school day, Ms. Jasmin was the lead teacher for the new ballet program she had brought to the school. As a former dancer herself, she remembered the amazing life lessons she gained when practicing and performing and wanted to afford similar opportunities at her new school. The twenty-seven students who showed up every Tuesday were already showing so much progress. They were becoming flexible and durable as they stretched and flexed every week. As they *listened to Ms. Jasmin give them commands in French, they responded by speaking to her with their dance.*

What stories can you tell? What experiences shaped who you are? Where do your values come from? And how does school fit into your current identity? Were you shaped by the lessons your teachers taught or by the experiences you walked through? What's the purpose of it all?

Chapter 2

"Do as I did. It worked for me." Does this advice have any merit?

Katelynn's Thoughts:

I'm going to hijack this question with a phrase that has the same sentiment, and that I hear incredibly often. Each time I hear it, I'm not really sure what to say because I wholeheartedly disagree with it.

"Let's not reinvent the wheel."

Now, before I ostracize anyone, I have to be straightforward—I've said this many times before, usually in reference to something in the educational field. It wasn't until a friend of mine pointed out to me how absolutely ridiculous it is, that I stopped using it altogether and began feeling annoyed every time I heard it.

Experience matters. But if the only reason we have for doing something is that we've always done it that way, we've *got* to re-evaluate what we're doing. If our only reason for continuing to do something the same way is that we want to avoid the work, that is absolutely not a good reason.

Sometimes, the wheel needs reinventing. As we learn more, as new research becomes available, as we grow in our understanding, we can apply this evolution to our approach. We can incorporate new technologies, we can eradicate harmful practices, we can utilize better, more effective strategies—all of which will require a little reinvention.

Doing things the same way they've always been done is not the right approach. Tried and true methods do exist, and we should consider them as viable options, but only if the reasoning is still sound. Only if, after careful consideration and application of our new understanding, it still remains just as powerful as before. And only if there is not something better, something more compelling, waiting to be discovered.

I don't say this to make more work for an already overworked profession. I say it knowing that educators are professionals. We are highly qualified, dedicated professionals who are constantly learning. All that learning should not, cannot, be done in vain. We must use it, apply it, and adapt our work to meet the needs of an ever-changing population: children.

We have the capacity to make monumental changes, not only in students' lives, but also to the education system as a whole. We have the power to dismantle institutionalized racism in schools, to take on ineffective and outdated grading practices, to create learning experiences that honor and value each of our kids and their experiences... but to do all that, we're going to need a little reinvention. So let's not shy away from it to do what we've always done. Let's jump in and get inventing.

~

"Do as I did. It worked for me." Does this advice have any merit?

Dave's Thoughts:

I run. I run a lot. I mean, I am no world champion, but I run. In the last decade, I have logged more than 13,000 miles, run six marathons, and burned through about fifty pairs of shoes. I am not fast. I don't win any trophies, but I run anyway.

When I run, I am able to clear my head and get lost in my thoughts. I have had some of my greatest ideas while all alone on a backcountry road putting in the miles. When I run, I am increasing my cardiovascular fitness and overall fitness. I could argue that running has helped shape me into the educator I am today. Running allows me a chance to breathe and think. Running consistently allows me to stay mentally fresh. Running keeps me healthy so that I can show up for work each and every day. Running works for me.

Imagine now, that this fall, on your first day back to school, I come to your school district and introduce myself to your staff, including the fact that I am a runner and my belief that running has helped shape me into the educator I am today. I then follow up my introduction with the news that your district is allowing me to enhance the teacher evaluation process in your district and I am creating the following expectation. "This year you will be evaluated on your ability to run like me. In May, we will run an educator marathon. In order for you to receive an "effective" evaluation label, you must finish your marathon, a full 26.2 miles, in a time similar to my average of about four hours. If you beat my time, you earn a 'highly effective.' If you finish slower than me, you earn a minimally effective label. Fail to show up and you receive no credit."

During this speech, I make the case that I am a successful educator. I have a doctorate degree. I have worked as a teacher, a building administrator, a central office administrator, a higher ed. professor, author, and speaker. I have won state and national awards, and I firmly believe part of that success is rooted in the fact that I run. I brainstorm when I run. I reflect when I run. I am healthy and am able to show up for work because I run, so if you want to be a successful educator, you need to run.

I know this sounds ludicrous. I also know that if something like this were actually attempted by me, a grievance would be filed with the teachers' union before I even left the stage. Some may say that running has nothing to do with teaching. Others may complain that they have a disadvantage because they have never run a day in their life. Others may have physical limitations. Maybe the PE teachers would be excited thinking they finally have an evaluation model that meets their needs, but most others would see this for what it is, a completely arbitrary and subjective performance review based on my limited experience and not on an objective review of evidence. They would argue that my expectations are not equitable and are not centered around what matters most.

The problem is, we often do something similar in our classrooms when we determine how we will evaluate our students. We often think back on our own school experiences and come up with criteria based more on what worked for us when we were students than by objectively reviewing the standards and determining what quality evidence of student mastery really looks like.

We tell our students that their grades will be impacted by when their assignments are turned in, the color of ink that is used, the spelling of words on the page, or my personal favorite, whether the hairy edges are cut off of the page when ripped out of a spiral notebook. We justify our grading decisions by making claims that if students really cared about their grades, then they would put forth the effort to play the game of school by our rules, because after all, "It worked for us".

The truth of the matter is this: as I write this, I am a forty-four-year-old father of four kids, who has worked in two states and five school districts. I have struggled with depression and anxiety. It took me twenty-two years to pay off my financial aid and get out of debt. I have my own share of personal demons. My goal is not to create other educators who are exact replicas of me but to help others reach their full potential to do more than I ever imagined. I want you to be more successful than I am. I want you to make better decisions than I did, to be better than I ever was, which means you have to follow a different path. Measuring your success by your ability to do what I did only limits you to be what I am, not what you can be. Sure running helps me, but that does not mean it will help you. If I want to really help you be a better educator, the feedback I provide to you should be objective, specific, and focused on what you do as an educator. Similarly, if you want to help your students be better learners, their grades, their shorthand version of feedback, should be focused on objective measures of their learning progression and mastery, not our arbitrary attempts to make smaller versions of ourselves.

We know that what we grade we value and what we value we teach. This year, as you examine your grading practices, pay special attention to what is measured and what is assessed to be sure that your policies do not limit your students but instead allow them to get an accurate evaluation of their progress in reaching their potential, not yours.

"Do as I did. It worked for me." Does this advice have any merit?

 **A Penny for My Thoughts:**

"Do as I did. It worked for me." Does this advice have any merit?

 **A Penny for Their Thoughts:**

Chapter 3

Whose version of the real world are we preparing kids for? Is it our job to prepare kids for "the real world"?

Katelynn's Thoughts:

Accountability is important. In classrooms across the world, there are measures put into place that are designed to hold students accountable for their actions. Teachers explain this necessity to their students, falling back on a similar line of thinking. Our reasoning? In the real world they will be expected to have this responsibility, they will be held to account, and when they get there, they won't have a safety net. They will have deadlines and expectations, and their bosses at their jobs will not be lenient or forgiving.

I held this belief. I shared this belief with my students... frequently. What could possibly be wrong with telling my kids that I was helping prepare them for the real world? The problem with this is the language that's being used to tell our students about the importance of accountability.

Our students' worlds are real. The problems they are facing in school, at home, within themselves are real. The joys and successes they experience are real. Their worlds are just as real as any of our adult ones. Yes, they are different, but that doesn't make them any less real.

Looking back, I am shocked that I never considered the implication of my words. I can remember back to when I was in seventh grade, dealing with problems that are still, to this day, some of the most difficult I have faced. Had a teacher belittled my issues, citing that the "real world" would not accept my late assignment, I would have immediately shut down. I would have lost respect for that teacher and would've been less likely to listen in the future. It would have been difficult for me to engage. Because I would have felt that this person (who had no idea what was happening with me) was judging my experience as less real. Simply because I was just a kid. Is this how we want our students to feel in our classrooms? I can confidently say that none of us has that goal in mind when we interact with our students.

When we consistently tell our students we are preparing them for the real world, we are discounting the current experiences they are having. We are telling them, in not so many words, that what they are going through is not as meaningful because they are not living in the *real world*. We are preparing them for their futures. We are preparing them for the challenges and obstacles that lie ahead of them. And yes, adults do have many rigid standards set for them within their careers. But that's just the thing—they are adults. We do not teach adults. We have a classroom full of children who need to be encouraged, supported, guided, and loved. The nature of our job is to give them the resources and tools necessary to face these challenges and come out the other side stronger and successful.

In addition to the language being used, the expectation of our students to behave as adults is unfair. Rather than explain to them that the real world is unforgiving, we must show them to be empathetic and considerate individuals who accept responsibility for their choices and actions. This is not to say that students should not be held accountable—they absolutely should. But we need to rethink how we teach accountability. Instead of consequences and punishments, start a conversation. Open the door to discuss the motivation behind the behavior. Ask questions, discover the meaning behind the action, and provide support, guidance, or advice. Develop a system of support and a new way of doing things so this student is successful in the future and feels valued in the classroom.

For example, when a student repeatedly misses deadlines for homework or other important assignments in class, it can be tempting to assign a consequence and chalk it up to laziness or apathy, utilizing that consequence as a *wake up call*. But what if, instead of the consequence, we asked the student to tell us about their situation—what was the cause of the missed deadlines. Are they struggling with organization? Do they feel overwhelmed? Are they having trouble with a friend and it's impacting their focus? By getting to the deeper root of the issue, we build the relationship up (instead of harming it), and we can use it as an opportunity to offer suggestions or support. We can take the time to help set up a planner or an agenda, go over the resources available when an issue with a friend comes up, or even just be a trusted adult who really, truly listens.

Our students come to us each and every day a sum of their experiences. Some of them are more hardened than others, some are more innocent and sweet, some are difficult to reach. But all of them have experiences outside of our walls. Real experiences. Meaningful experiences. Experiences that have shaped who they are. Experiences that may stay with them for the rest of their lives. It is up to us educators to help shape who they will become, and it starts by reconsidering how we hold them accountable for their choices.

∽

Dave's Thoughts:

I'm an 80s kid. I was born in 1977 and spent the bulk of my childhood in the greatest decade ever. I wore knee-high striped socks with my short shorts. I listened to Michael Jackson, Tiffany, and Guns and Roses. My beloved Detroit Pistons were winning championships for me, and the Detroit Tigers were World Series champions.

My childhood was filled with kickball, bike rides, and Mr. Wizard. Today, I have four children of my own. My oldest child, a teenager, wears shorts that fall below his knees and a hoodie every day. My kids watch television shows downloaded from the Internet. Kickball has been replaced by E-sports, and my favorite sports teams probably won't even make the playoffs this year.

My childhood was a long time ago and a lot has changed since then. As a child I had no Internet, no home computer, no clue what my future would hold. I believed I would grow up to be a truck driver, a meteorologist, and a Navy Seal. Today, my kids dream of being vloggers and YouTube stars. My kids have no idea what childhood was like forty years ago, and back then I could never have imagined what childhood would look like today. Similarly, forty years ago I had no idea what adulthood would be like when I actually got there, and neither did any of the adults I surrounded myself with.

Many of us have heard the statistics describing the number of new jobs that will exist in twenty years, jobs that aren't even in our imaginations today. The reality is, we have no idea how many new jobs will exist because we have no idea what new technologies will be developed, what new consumer demands will be created, and what services will be required.

Knowing about this uncertainty, we, as educators, still try to tell our students why all the content we are exposing them to is important and how it will help them in the future. In reality, all we are doing is telling these students, children with uncertain futures, how that content has helped prepare us for our present, which may or may not be relevant to their future.

It's important to ask ourselves daily, "Are we preparing students for *their* futures or for *our* past?"

As educators, our job is to contribute to the future. We have jobs that others try to measure in moments of time through daily observations and summative assessments, when, truly, our success can only be measured in generations. If what we are presenting to our students cannot endure, we must ask if it is something we should be spending our time on at all.

Now, don't get me wrong. Standards-based learning (SBL) is a key to achieving success. Clearly articulating objectives and assessing based on growth and progress, mastery, and proficiency are critical components of lasting learning and enduring education, but none are the silver bullet. I have built my professional reputation—my career—on articulating the importance and relevance of focused, standards-based learning and grading. But even I know that SBL, as it is often described, is only a piece of the puzzle.

In education, we are often guilty of seeking the Holy Grail or a magic pill to cure all and fix what others perceive to be broken. We attend a conference and hear one educator tell a story of what has worked in her classroom, with her kids, in her community, and jump on board to try to replicate that program in our school with our kids in our way and expect the same results. We chase programs over people. We search for curriculum over creativity. When we don't see immediate results, we drift back to the status quo and wonder if the next blog we read, the next professional development seminar we attend, or the next team meeting will reveal the answer we have been looking for.

We need to stop looking for THE answer and instead continue to look for AN answer, realizing that we have millions of children in a multitude of environments, with countless unknown futures who all require something a little bit different.

I currently work in a state that has adopted College and Career Readiness Standards. This is such a great idea, yet so often misapplied and misinterpreted by the very people responsible for their implementation. I am currently in my third decade as a professional educator. When I look back on my first year and compare it to this year, I can honestly say I was a mess when I began. I had no idea what I was doing almost thirty years ago.

Prior to becoming a teacher, I attended a great teacher preparation university, Central Michigan University (Go, Fire Up, Chips!), and had a diverse student teaching experience and a phenomenal mentor. But despite all of that, the only thing that could properly prepare me for my career was my career. This is why veteran teachers make more money than first year teachers. It is not because older teachers are worth more; it is because they've had more experiences, and we assume they've had the opportunity to refine and grow their skill sets as a result.

We understand that experience in the career is what prepares us for the career. The same is true of almost every career you can imagine. Whether it is professional sports, education, engineering, public safety, or medicine, often the only thing that truly makes you ready for your career is your career ... and a lot of grace offered to you by those you work with as you make mistakes along the way.

The same is true of college readiness. When I look back on my first year of college, I wonder how in the world I am still alive. I graduated high school with a 3.8 grade point average. I was the student council president. I competed in sports and Model United Nations. I was a self-described model high school student, yet my first year of college was a disaster. I may have had some book smarts when I entered, but I was lacking a lot of "not so common" sense.

When we say we are preparing students to be ready for college and career, are we measuring this based on their short-term retention of academic facts, or are we really providing them with skills and opportunities that will transcend the safety of their

K-12 school system and lead them towards long-term success and happiness, regardless of what the future holds? Are we giving them the persistence, confidence, humility, and curiosity that will lead to future learning, or are we giving students the answers to questions that exist today without the ability to question the answers that we believe will exist tomorrow?

As educators we must get back to embracing that if we are indeed trying to set our students up for success in their careers and college that we are responsible for teaching skills, not just content. We are not just in the test prep business; we are in the experience creating business. Yes, we want students to learn, but real learning, learning that lasts, has nothing to do with memorizing facts and figures. Learning that lasts is all about making memories and creating experiences. Great teachers recognize this, and great leaders encourage this.

We have to focus on the future, but when our eyes are only on what is to come, we run the risk of losing sight of who is in front of us today. Kids are not waiting for their lives to begin. They are living their lives today. There is a difference between teaching kids and teaching future adults and knowing this may just be THE difference maker you have been looking for.

~

Whose version of the real world are we preparing kids for?

A Penny for My Thoughts:

Whose version of the real world are we preparing kids for?

A Penny for Their Thoughts:

Chapter 4

Should schools be a place for fun?

Katelynn's Thoughts:

There tend to be two camps of thought on this topic. One is that school is a student's job. It's a place for them to learn responsibility and do what is expected of them each day. The other set of beliefs is that school should be a place for students to explore their identities and interests, discovering their passion and future goals. In both cases, students are expected to learn and grow as they progress through each level of their education.

Personally, I believe that if we want to encourage real, lasting learning, we have to make it relevant and meaningful for kids. They have to see themselves in our curriculum, and see their education as their own. We can accomplish this through the inclusion of voice and choice in our classrooms.

When we incorporate voice and choice, we empower our learners. Giving students a say in their education—whether that be in the process, product, or content— is what personalized learning is all about. It's a lot simpler than it sounds. And it's a lot simpler to put into practice than I originally thought. In my own experience, I incrementally made some changes to my practice that made all the difference.

I started by adjusting some of my language arts units to incorporate more student choice. I began with the basics: letting kids choose a topic to write about or a book to read from a menu. Then giving them options or topics to assess their proficiency at our learning targets. As I became more comfortable with it, the freedom I offered became more sophisticated. Students had the opportunity to pace out the work the way they wanted, attending mini lessons when they needed them. I began giving them completely open-ended assessments, providing only the learning targets and challenging them to show me what they knew.

It was hard at first to give up the notion of control. But, in the end, that's all it was... an idea. Once I cleared up my own misconception that my students couldn't possibly handle this kind of freedom, once I got over the fact that it was actually possible to support students moving at their own pace (I mean, think about it, you probably already do this), my classroom buzzed with learning.

Kids were working on their reading and writing skills in earnest. They were creating products for assessment that were mind-blowing. Poems were being written, iMovies were casted and produced, skits were being performed, games were being coded. It was amazing the talent, the ability, I had in my room. Kids were flourishing under this kind of guidance.

From that, I was inspired to write a new kind of unit, one completely focused on helping students find their voices. We had always given speeches in our sixth-grade ELA classes, and the kids always did well on them. It usually ended up being a challenging, but fun experience for them. I knew I wanted them to give a speech. I knew I wanted it to involve research and information writing. I just didn't quite know how to structure it so that we could accomplish these important learning goals, while still empowering them with choice and voice. So I took to the Internet. I reflected. I pondered our standards. I researched.

And I stumbled across this quote attributed to civil rights leader, Howard Thurman, as I was looking. *"Don't ask what the world needs. Ask what makes you come alive, and go do it. Because what the world needs is people who have come alive."*

As I read this quote to myself, I couldn't help but think about how my job, the job of all educators, is to help our students become the people they will ultimately be. To guide them in their lives, helping them develop skills for their futures and inspiring them to find what they love. And, with that, The Passion Project was born.

I've now taught this unit for several years, and each time, it is just as powerful as the last. For four weeks in my classroom, my students conduct research, write expository pieces, and practice informational speaking standards. They create multimedia presentations. They learn skills to engage an audience. They discover the power of credible sources. They learn to structure an informative piece of writing so it makes sense. In short, this unit includes some serious learning.

There is frustration, as there typically is in learning something new. (If you've ever taught kids to research using something that isn't a basic Google search, you know the frustration wasn't just from them.) But there's also a lot of excitement, which is something I love to see when I've created a new learning experience.

This unit was built on the idea that I want to help my students find what they love, learn as much as they can about it, and then set a goal for themselves that involves this passion. That goal could be to make a career of it or involving it, to start a service project, to take up a new hobby, to create a club, or really anything they want it to be. The bigger piece is that they find a way to do something with what they learn, and then share it with the class in a speech.

The lesson that this unit taught me was an important one. One that influenced the trajectory of my career and my philosophy of education. It showed me the power of fully letting the control pass to my students. During the first Passion Project, I witnessed the transformative quality of empowering students not *just* to choose what they want to learn about, but to find a way to develop their passions. I watched my students become ignited and invested in their learning process. They cared about the work because it was about their own futures, interests, and aspirations. We saw together how important it is to discover how to do something with what you love. And we had **fun**.

So when I think about whether or not school should be fun, I think we're asking ourselves a different question. Are we providing a space in our school where kids can explore? Are we giving them room to discover their identities? Are we honoring their voices and passions? Are we providing the type of learning environment that helps them **become**? Are our students able to see themselves in the curriculum and classrooms? Because I truly believe that the answer to every single one of those questions should be yes.

∾

Dave's Thoughts:

A few years ago I had the amazing opportunity to attend the graduation ceremony at a private college where I had the privilege to teach as an adjunct professor. The college I worked for had an open enrollment policy and the belief that "every student deserves the chance to try." Most major universities have a selection criteria enabling them to only select the students who have already displayed evidence that they believe will lead to future success. The open enrollment philosophy of the college where I worked allowed for a more diverse student body, as many students were first-generation college students who may not have shown high levels of academic achievement earlier in life. But when given a chance to earn a degree, the thought was, they just might find equal footing and a chance to climb the ladder to career success.

The United States, as a whole, is a country that claims to believe that all can achieve, all can make it; all that's needed is hard work, effort, and a goal. Many claim to believe that anyone can climb the ladder to success, if only they take it upon themselves to work hard enough to get there. I agree, however, the often misunderstood and ignored flaw in this thought process is the belief that we all begin on the same rung of the ladder, when in reality, this is far from the truth for so many.

Poverty in the United States is concentrated. It is not widespread and not equally dispersed. For full transparency, I am a middle-aged white man who lives in the suburbs. I have a middle-class income and live in a neighborhood that I consider safe and secure.

I spent the first twenty years of my career working in schools where the students, the staff, and the community looked like me, acted like me, and sounded like me. As a result, I often thought that my view of the world was an accurate description of the entire world. I used to believe that anyone could have a life just like mine if they just worked hard enough. I spent a decade of my career working as a school principal. For full transparency, most of the schools I worked in were in the suburbs, filled with students originating from upper-middle class homes.

31

However, before becoming an assistant superintendent and leaving school-based leadership, I was given the opportunity to lead a school that was unlike any I had ever served in before. This amazing little school was not located in my neighborhood. It was not a school I was familiar with. The kids did not look like me and the families did not look like mine. The students came from high levels of poverty. More than 90% of the students at the school came from homes that qualified for free lunch. We would send home backpacks filled with food to feed families on the weekend. Dozens of our students faced challenges like having a parent in jail, and a large percentage of the students lived with an adult other than their biological parent.

Working in this building, serving these students, was an opportunity and a blessing. My job was to change destinies by changing realities. When I accepted the job, I felt my responsibility was to play savior, to pull kids out of their current circumstance and show them that they could have a life just like mine. Within days, however, I realized how arrogant and egocentric that mindset was. My job was not to create students who embraced my life, but instead, my charge was to become a part of their lives.

Before becoming a principal, I was introduced to one of my heros, Dr. Nelson Maylone. Dr. Maylone is well known in the state of Michigan for his work on identifying the correlation between student socio-economic status (SES) and academic achievement. It is well established in educational research that a key factor impacting student achievement in schools is the SES level the student lives in at home. There is, however, a way to address this problem. Dr. Maylone, in his research, was able to demonstrate that success on state end-of-year tests was more correlated to home zip code and household income than classroom instructional design.

First, let me be clear that a parent's paycheck is not a magic pill for student learning. Just because money is going into a bank account does not mean that lasting learning is being absorbed by a child. So what does it mean? When a child lives in poverty, there are many factors that a school may not have power over. We cannot control family dynamics, past experiences, or parental expectations. Some parents have higher expectations than you. Some have lower. Some parents work multiple jobs to make ends meet, some stay home. Some parents believe in the power of education. Some are holding on to past hurts of a system that let them down. Each of these aspects does have an impact on success, but there is something schools can do that is so often missed. There are things we can control.

In many states, schools that have students with struggling achievement results are mandated into strict schedules, tight curriculum controls, and focused instruction. Student downtime is limited. Everything is mapped, planned, and structured. I understand why, but I believe this is a flawed plan.

I could share the data that demonstrates that national SAT scores are actually lower now than they were fifteen years ago, in all subgroups and populations. I could share the latest PISA results that show American students further behind their international counterparts today than they were a decade ago. Both would show that current practices are not working, but I won't share that. Instead, I'll share an observation.

Yes, students from poverty tend to score lower on academic achievement tests than their peers in more affluent communities, but poverty alone is not the cause. When students live in communities with high poverty, students also tend to live in areas of high crime (Anser et. al., 2020). In some areas of high crime, parents are not as willing to let their students get outside and enjoy the community. Instead, in an effort to keep children safe, they are often kept indoors where they are not afforded the opportunity to explore the world around them—a decision my own parents made for me when I was a young child living in a subsidized housing project.

I spent the first twenty years of my career working in schools where the students, the staff, and the community looked like me, acted like me, and sounded like me. As a result, I often thought that my view of the world was an accurate description of the entire world. I used to believe that anyone could have a life just like mine if they just worked hard enough. In 2015, however, my entire world view shifted when I was asked to lead a school, a staff, and a community that was nothing like anything I had ever been around before. The school I was asked to lead was located in the panhandle of Florida, a location just two miles from the beach in the Sunshine State, yet so many of my students had spent the vast majority of their days protected inside of a building, whether at home or at school, never getting the chance to learn from play. My elementary-aged students were often asked to help raise their siblings, asked to make adult decisions daily, and often had no chance to embrace so many of the joys of childhood that I took for granted and often take for granted with my own biological children.

Today, because of my job, I get the chance to travel quite a bit. In recent years, my work has brought me to communities that are suburban, rural, and urban. I also acknowledge that my time in each of these communities is limited and my perspective is biased. I bring my own thoughts, beliefs, and values with me. As much as I try to lead from a research-based mindset, I often drift back towards thinking that my own experiences are the only research I need. I take my own beliefs and actions and project them out towards others. For example, last spring while out of town visiting and supporting a few school districts, I was able to witness a number of communities in small town America, communities that have schools with high levels of student academic success. In each of these towns, I saw one commonality. Kids. Kids running around and playing OUTSIDE. I remember smiling and thinking, "This is pure 'Americana.' This is where I would want to raise my kids." I did not see kids sitting on porches reading books. I did not see kids lined up outside of libraries and museums. I saw kids who attend schools with great achievement results being allowed outside to play. I saw kids running around without parental supervision. I saw kids falling off of bikes and getting back on. I saw kids riding skateboards. I saw kids swinging and sliding. Kids playing with kids. Kids speaking with kids. Kids learning with kids.

My bias of thinking, "This is the American way," is completely slanted towards my own experiences, but research also supports the notion that play may be a bigger contributor to student academic success than many of the other strategies we try to implement in our struggling schools. Students who live in poverty may often miss out on the ability to have organic, playful experiences with peers, when this activity leads to more learning than anything else we can do with our kids (Engle & Black, 2008). Kids need to play. There is a difference between learning to play and playing to learn. Playing to learn, playing for joy, playing for purpose, that is the difference-maker (Ciolan, 2013).

So yes, I believe kids need to have fun in order to learn. In some of our communities, schools are literally the safest space available for our kids, safer than neighborhood parks, safer than front yards, safer than any other public space. If we want our kids to thrive, we need to let them go outside and play. If we want our students to thrive, we must give them opportunities to play. We need to create a safe place, free from worldly problems, a place where kids can fall down and get back up. We need to create a place where students can argue and make up. We need to create a place where students can create, solve, make, and grow. You can do as I did in my school and choose to purchase Lego, PlayDoh, Big Blue Blocks, and puzzles in lieu of worksheets and drill and kill activity books. You can volunteer to go into your school community and supervise the play-grounds. You can host Open Gyms, block parties, or gaming clubs. Or perhaps you just want to choose to double up on recess time each day knowing that kids will learn more here than perhaps anywhere else.

Is poverty a real burden for many students? ABSOLUTELY. Is it a complex and multi-faceted problem? OF COURSE....but it is not an excuse to eliminate all aspects of fun, joy, and play from our schools. Kids deserve a chance to try. Kids deserve the opportunity to begin climbing the same ladder as your kids. Kids need to learn and experiment and fail and grow—which can all be accomplished through play. While many schools choose to focus on extended days, more focused curricular demands, and enhanced instructional interventions to help students who may have a history of perceived underperformance, I believe, if we simply get out of the way, provide opportunities for kids to be kids, to play, to grow, and learn, in a safe and supportive environment, we may be able to actually level the playing field in more tangible ways than ever before.

~

Should schools be a place for fun?

A Penny for My Thoughts:

Should schools be a place for fun?

A Penny for Their Thoughts:

Chapter 5

Is it our job to teach the "soft skills"?

Katelynn's Thoughts:

Any time we want our students to learn a new skill, master new content, or achieve a new goal, educators make sure they do several things.

First, we activate prior knowledge or any background information the students might have about the skill or concept. We help our students draw on previous experiences, learning or life, that might apply to the new situation and help them better understand it.

Then, we begin teaching the new content. We start with the basics, the foundational skills, that are core to mastery. As the skills increase in difficulty, we provide continued instruction and support, offering scaffolding to help our students achieve independent understanding. We check their progress along the way, offering feedback to help them continue their growth. When failures or setbacks arise, we praise students for taking a risk, and help them get back on track by providing targeted assistance or lessons based on their gaps in knowledge. If a student has a misconception or doesn't quite master the skill, we circle back, remediate, and provide more instruction to help them get there.

After we've taught the new concept, we check for student mastery. We ask that students demonstrate the skills through application, and we offer praise when they do. We celebrate the accomplishment in the moment, but we know that it's possible we'll have to revisit that same skill in the future. When needed, we review the information and reteach to ensure our students maintain their mastery.

But in our classrooms, we do not just teach content. We teach **people.** As a result, we do much more than teach skills. We manage behaviors, hold students accountable, promote social emotional development, and so much more. Often, these are new concepts for our students. So why in the world would we just expect students to know them? Why would we not take the time to teach it, just like anything else?

When it comes to the soft skills, it often necessitates a similar approach to teaching content. We must activate prior knowledge and experience, teach the skill, progress monitor, and reteach when necessary.

I teach sixth graders, and in our district, these eleven-year-olds are entering middle school for the very first time. They are coming into an entirely new environment, a new building, multiple teachers and classrooms, and a whole lot of other new structures. It's a lot to contend with, especially for a kid! That's why we start our year with two days devoted solely to developing some core skills for success: self-regulation, accountability, organization, and self-care. We talk about systems we've used in the past that worked, what adjustments we might need to make, and we share ways that we take time to recharge and focus on ourselves. These two days are great for building community, but they also help my students draw on their experience *before* things get tough and overwhelming. And, what's more, it gives us a chance to find some common understanding of what we might need to be successful in middle school. As the year progresses, we don't have these isolated lessons anymore. Instead, we integrate reminders and moments into our day. For example, students in my class have a lot of independent time to write, read, collaborate, or meet with me. During these stretches of time, they recognize when they need to take a break and they do! If they are struggling to recognize that need, I can meet them where they are and give some gentle reminders about self-care and regulation—encouraging them to take the break they need to reset.

Whether students need to learn positive behavior, coping skills, accountability, or the like, we have a responsibility to teach it. Just like we wouldn't expect them to come into our classrooms with a fully developed knowledge of essay writing, we can't expect them to have mastered soft skills without instruction.

Dave's Thoughts:

The soft skills are often the hard skills.

I am a father to four amazing kids, and if I am being honest, most of the time I think I am a pretty good dad. I take each of my kids out for one-on-one time. I smile and laugh. I play tickle tag, baseball, and Barbies, but I have my struggles.

I hate seeing my kids get upset. I hate seeing them struggle. I want each of them to feel victorious and confident. As a speaker and writer, I often tell educators elsewhere how important it is to allow students to fail so they can receive feedback, become innovators, and grow. Yet in my own home, I struggle to practice what I preach. I often hold my kids back from amazing learning moments by focusing on quick smiles more than enduring triumphs.

My oldest child is now sixteen. He is amazing. He is a typical boy who spends hours playing video games with friends. He loves soccer. He is sweet, kind, and forgiving, but I also know I held him back for a long time from seeing even more success. When Cameron, my son, was younger I did EVERYTHING for him, and it shows today.

When Cameron was an infant, I was a classroom teacher and coach. He was able to come watch many of the games where I was standing on the sidelines coaching, and he often came to visit my classroom. As he grew, I made the decision to quit coaching the kids in my school so that I could begin coaching his teams. I coached him in t-ball, basketball, and soccer. Cam is a great athlete, but when I was on the sidelines, it didn't always show. I coached him for seven years until my schedule just got too intense, and I could no longer commit to being at every game and practice. I had to let my coaching responsibilities go to someone else. He needed to be coached by people he did not call "dad", and it was then that Cam began to flourish. As a soccer player, Cam scored his first goal a few years ago, at the first game I didn't coach, and as a matter of fact, I didn't even attend. He went on to score six goals that year.

I don't believe this was because he received better coaching that year, although that may be the case. But instead, as Cam told me, he didn't have to look over his shoulder while playing to see if Dad approved. He was free to just play.

Cameron is now sixteen, but has only been a tennis shoe wearing kid for six years...at least to school. He was lucky enough to attend school in Florida for a few years where he could wear flip flops, because he was nervous about his shoes coming untied when I wasn't around to help. You see, I tied Cam's shoes for him until he was ten. This wasn't because he didn't have the ability to do it himself; it was just that when he was really young, I hated to see him struggle and would do it for him and that just became the way things were done. It's the same reason I would help him with his homework every night, help make his bed in the mornings, cut up his food, etc... Because I wanted him to feel successful and happy all the time. I actually cost him the chance to learn and figure things out on his own.

As a leader in a public school system, I see, everyday, others who struggle just like I do. Adults working in schools love kids and want to see them shine and smile, and often, as a result, hold back their opportunity to really grow and develop. We answer every question they have. We run to their assistance when they struggle with opening their lockers. We switch their schedules when they have a teacher they don't like. We kneel down at their desks and give them the answers to complex math problems, and then state, "Does that make sense?" as an attempt to validate to ourselves that the child now understands the work we have done for them.

As a leader I know I have fallen victim to this with the adults that work with me too. I have heard about the value of Servant Leadership and have used this as the defense for doing everything for some. I call parents. I substitute in classrooms. I discipline students. I analyze data. I have found myself at times doing so much to help that I actually may hurt. Instead of teaching adults how to fish I often bring the fish directly to them. I want to feel needed. I want to feel important, and as such find myself doing instead of guiding.

As I look back on my last twenty plus years in education, and the last sixteen years as a dad, I have many moments I am extremely proud of. I have had some epic successes, but I know fearing failure has been one of my biggest failures. I know that as I look into the future towards my next twenty years, if I want to have even more successes, I have to allow others to have even more failures. This is where innovation comes from. This is where growth comes from. This is where lasting learning comes from.

Is it our job to teach the "soft skills"?

A Penny for My Thoughts:

Is it our job to teach the "soft skills"?

A Penny for Their Thoughts:

Part Two

Grades

[greyds] a degree or step in a scale, as of rank, advancement, quality, value, or intensity

— Dictionary.com

"Grades are communication, not compensation."

— Rick Wormeli — *Fair Isn't Always Equal*

"The tests used to evaluate schools often assess what students bring to school, not what they are taught once they arrive."

— W. James Popham — *Assessment Literacy*

Many of us have a story or a moment of realization with grades—an epiphany if you will—when we realized that the points are the point or even that the points are pointless. These stories can range from teacher-centric, individual snippets of clarity to ones with greater, more serious consequences. Each of us have had these moments. Moments of heartache. Moments of embarrassment. Whether you have had one of these moments or not, we hope that our stories provide the catalyst for the conversations and subsequent actions that can impact destinies.

The Points are Pointless—Katelynn's story

I was a newer teacher, only a few years into my career, and I was a staunch believer in traditional grading systems. Points and percentages were my preference, and I frequently hailed their praises as a concrete, black and white, objective grading system. As I started my graduate coursework, I began taking classes on assessment and learned more about different ways of measuring student progress and proficiency.

It was a year into my Master's degree that I was sitting at my desk in my classroom, grabbing a Flair pen to begin grading my students' most recent language arts assignment. We had been working on grammar, and I gave several practice assignments for my students to work on throughout the week. On each sheet, students were expected to complete a variety of tasks to continue working on the skills we had learned about in class. By the end of the week, they had completed several of these tasks and I was gearing up to grade them all.

I flipped through each page, totaling the number of questions. I made some questions two points and others five points, and still others only one point, depending on how "much" I was expecting them to do. For a few of the questions, I added a point or two for writing in complete sentences. For other questions, I decided to add a point for using end punctuation. Sometimes, I even added a point for correctly following the directions at the top of the page because I didn't think they would read the directions or follow them on that activity.

When I finished doing the math, the sum total was 127 points. I was irritated that it wasn't a nice round 130, so I decided to add 3 points for correct capitalization. As I went to add this 130 point assignment to the gradebook, it hit me like a brick wall. The points I assigned were utterly and completely pointless.

I had randomly and subjectively decided each question's "worth" as I flipped through the pages, based on my personal interpretation of how difficult the questions were. I assigned point values that were fair according to me and me alone, and arbitrarily determined that sometimes I would increase the value of a question for an additional skill that I deemed valuable. And, the biggest tell of all, I simply decided that I would add three more points to the overall assignment just because I didn't want the total points to be an odd number. If I was able to do that, for seemingly no reason other than the neatness of my gradebook, then this entire system was completely messed up.

My methods were random at best and only known by me. But it wasn't just my methods—it was the entire structure of grades and points and percentages. I realized at that moment that nothing about it was clear, objective, or valid. It was incredibly unreliable and had another teacher looked at the same assignment, they could have come up with a completely different point value than I did.

This small moment changed the way I viewed assessment and grading immensely. The system I had viewed as concrete, black and white, and completely objective was actually... not. This 127 point assignment and the lesson it taught me has stuck with me years later. Each time I consider different approaches to grading or assessment, I'm reminded of sitting at my desk, Flair pen in hand, finally realizing that the points are pointless.

The Point is The Point–Dave's story

Justin was an amazing student in my eighth-grade class. He was tall, athletic, and labeled as a "gifted student" by those who taught him before me. He came from an affluent family. His father was the personal attorney to the governor of my home state. For all intents and purposes, he was in a pretty amazing position to see success throughout his life.

It was late March and spring was beginning to emerge. Like most newer teachers, actually, like almost all teachers, I was beginning to see the light at the end of the tunnel and I was already preparing for the summer. The year had been a relative success with few speed bumps and I just had to make it a couple of more months.

At this point in my career, I was still using an overhead projector in my classroom, had lessons and worksheets filling up a filing cabinet, and rarely received messages from parents on the new platform called, e-mail, but Justin's dad, a man with access to technology and a knack for communication, sent me a message on a Friday afternoon, which I received during my planning period while watching March Madness basketball games on my classroom TV typically used for broadcasting Channel One news to students, requesting a conference the following Monday. I readily accepted, anticipating an easy conversation about an amazing kid.

Justin's father showed up in my classroom after school that Monday dressed in an impressive three-piece suit, clashing with my bright yellow t-shirt sporting the school mascot emblazoned across the front. He sat down across from my desk, in a student seat, clearly not intimidated by the power imbalance I had created when I sank into my oversized desk chair, and shook my hand while smiling. As he sat, he thanked me for my time and promised this conversation would only take a few minutes. As we began to talk, I felt like I was getting to know a new friend. He asked about my year. He wanted to know about my family and my background. He was full of charm. Then, after crossing his legs and leaning back, he asked me very calmly, "You know I work for the governor, right? You know her daughter is also in your class, right? You know, last week the governor and I were talking about you and how much both of our kids enjoy your class. But I just have to ask, do you think her daughter is smarter than my son?"

I hadn't been given an opportunity to respond to the earlier softball questions, but at this point, utilizing skills I am sure he had sharpened while practicing law, Justin's dad just waited, eager to hear how I answered. Fully aware now, that the man across from me was an attorney, I gave my best, defensive answer, "I'm sorry sir, but I cannot address the academic progress of another child, but I will tell you that I think Justin is amazing. As a matter of fact, he has a grade of 103% right now."

Justin's father and I entered into an amazing conversation over the next fifteen minutes that opened my eyes to the world of grading and just how arbitrary my feedback had been. Many of us have experienced conversations led by helicopter parents arguing for the one extra point in class, even though their child already has a grade beyond everyone else. This wasn't one of those conversations.

You see, Justin's dad had learned in talking to the governor that her daughter had a grade of 104%. After some good natured joking about how her daughter was obviously smarter than his son, Justin's father committed to having a talk with me, not about his son, completely, but about how teachers in general grade and evaluate all students. Justin had a sister, two years younger than he was, who missed a "gifted designation" in fifth grade, because her teacher issued her an 89% B+ in science, and not the requisite 90% A- needed to enter the program.

As we continued to talk, I was reminded that when we returned from the holiday break in January, I had requested students bring in Kleenex boxes and offered one point of extra credit for each box a student brought in. The governor's daughter brought five. Justin brought none. In the grand scheme of things, Justin's report card grade would be the same as the governor's daughter, an A+. The letter grade wasn't what mattered. The point was the point, a lesson I would be reminded of again fifteen years later when I was serving as an elementary school principal in an impoverished community in an attempt to turn a school around.

Javon was an 11-year-old third grader. In the state he lived in, and the state I had moved to, retention was mandatory for any student who failed to pass mathematics and reading. Javon had failed both his first time in third grade and math his second time through the grade level. Javon's third attempt at third grade was my first as his principal.

At the end of the school year, I received some concerning news. Teachers were required to share with me the names of any student who had not yet passed a required class, indicating possible retention. Javon was on the list.

According to his teacher, Javon had earned a 59% overall grade in math. A 60% was needed to pass. As a principal in his first year at a new school, in a new state, I had a decision to make. Was this going to be the hill I fought on? One point. He missed passing his math class by one point. Surely his teacher would show some compassion and just inflate his grade by one point. Countless conversations later, his teacher was not budging. She could not be convinced to change her calculation when his grade was based on his inability to do calculations. I could have dug deeper. I could have analyzed every assignment. I could have explored every task and every question used to calculate that 59%, but I chose to ignore it all. The 59% stuck. Javon was given an "F" and was slated to return in the fall as a 12-year-old third grader.

Javon never made it back to school. In August, two weeks before the first day of my second year, Javon was shot and killed. Earlier in the summer, this sweet third-grade boy began running drugs from his neighborhood to the one a few blocks away. He had been convinced that becoming a drug runner was the future that was destined for him, because school obviously wasn't working out.

As I sat in the church at Javon's funeral, I was overcome with guilt. I knew there were a number of factors that contributed to his fate, but I couldn't help but think that my unwillingness to fight was also a factor. Maybe if I had paid more attention to his grade. Maybe if I had chosen to really dig into it. Maybe. Maybe that one point could have been found. Maybe if I had actually learned my lesson from Justin years earlier I would have remembered that sometimes the point is the point.

∽

Whether you've had this moment yourself or not, we invite you to consider the practice of grading as we tackle some of the biggest questions that need answered.

Chapter 6

What is the purpose of a grade?

Katelynn's Thoughts:

When we consider grades, many of our minds go straight to a traditional system of letters, percents, and points. That is what we grew up with, what our experience was, and so it's our first reaction. But when we think more critically about it, what really is a grade? What does it exist to do? What, then, is the point of all those points?

A grade, at its core, is a mode of communication between the teacher and learner, or between the teacher and the learner's family. It is the way educators share the level of academic proficiency a student has achieved throughout the learning experience. When done well, a grade outlines a student's ability in a given academic area, noting the areas of strength or learning goals met and those objectives with room for improvement. When done, let's say, *not* well, it is an arbitrary value, obtained in a transactional manner, which is muddied with various components that are completely unrelated to academic proficiency.

By taking time to assign numbers to a student's learning, to give and take points away, what are we communicating about their progress? Does this grade offer any specific feedback on an academic skill? Does it give students an idea on how to improve? Does it offer a way for them to demonstrate new learning? Does it truly accomplish the purpose of a grade —which is, objectively, to report academic ability? I would contend that no, the traditional system does not match this purpose. Instead, grades are most often used to enforce compliance, to determine how well learners have molded to the subjective notion of a *good student*. And, in other cases, it creates a competition between students, using a literal and figurative scoreboard to help them measure their worth against each other.

When we look at grading reform, it is vital that we ensure our focus is on the true purpose behind a grade. That is, we must make sure our mindset has shifted towards communication of progress and that our model of assessment matches that idea.

There are many ways to accomplish this particular goal, and I would argue that there is no *one* right way. The right way, the best way, is the one that will work in your setting, in your district, with your students. That said, one approach that I have had great success with is skill-based proficiency rubrics. These rubrics are often quick to put together, allow for flexibility in implementation, and are clear outlines of what a student should be able to do. They focus on one skill at a time, clearly demonstrating to anyone who is interested, exactly where that student falls in their level of proficiency.

While this one method has worked particularly well for me, there are plenty of others that exist. Whatever method we choose, it is necessary that we ensure it meets our intended outcome and is in line with our purpose—to communicate a student's academic proficiency as clearly and objectively as possible.

RI.6.6 LEARNING PROGRESSION

	4 - Proficient	3 - Approaching	2 - Developing	1 - Beginning
RI.6.6 - Reading Information: Author's Purpose Determine an author's purpose in a text and explain how it is conveyed in the text.	Identified the author's purpose for writing a text. Explained how they know this is the author's purpose.	Identified the author's purpose for writing a text. *(Ex. The author wrote this text to inform us about WWII.)*	Did not identify the author's complete purpose for writing a text. *(Ex. The author wrote this text to inform.)*	Unable to identify the author's purpose for writing a text.

∼

Dave's Thoughts:

I am going to steal a quote from one of my heroes, a man who made me question all I was doing and why I was doing it, Rick Wormeli. "A grade is communication, not compensation."

Whether we use four-point rubrics, smiley face stickers, check marks, letter grades, or percentages, the grades we assign to students and the work they submit, communicate our values, our expectations, and our reactions to student quality. **What** we grade often tells as much of our story as **how** we grade. And yes, I meant OUR story, not their story.

In classrooms all across the United States, I have witnessed grading practices designed to create and communicate our values and our paths to success at the expense of allowing for true differentiation and student autonomy. When we assign points for participation, we are singling out and celebrating the extroverts at the expense of the introverts. When we disallow students to make corrections because they *should have worked harder the first time*, we diminish opportunities for growth and reflection. When we deduct points for tardiness, we place more value on our arbitrary deadlines than the life experiences of the students we are asked to support.

When we assign weighted measures indicating that "formative assessments" are ONLY worth 25%, we are making the statement that this evidence, the evidence we are claiming to use to inform our practice and guide our instruction, hence the term FORMATIVE, is not as high quality or as important as the "summative" tasks that count for the majority of a final grade.

So what is the purpose of a grade? Well, a grade is simply a shorthand approach to providing the feedback we believe others need to receive. A grade is simply a way to capture all of our thoughts on quality, performance, mastery, and growth and synthesized down to a single symbol that we hope everyone is able to interpret and understand. So as Rick Wormeli says, "A grade is communication," and the question is, are we communicating with enough feedback to allow for growth and progress or simply to assign a label and designation? But, I literally wrote an entire book on that

(*Making Assessment Work for Educators Who Hate Data but Love Kids*), so we can save that conversation for later. For now, though, I implore you to answer, what is the difference between a C+ and a B-? What can a student who earns an A do that a student who earns a B+ cannot? If your answers are simply based on points earned, then what you are communicating is that point collection matters more than learning, and if that is what you really believe, then your grades may be completely accurate. If that is not what you believe, if you believe learning matters more, what changes can you make today to help your student feedback be a better reflection of learning and growth?

~

What is the purpose of a grade?

A Penny for My Thoughts:

What is the purpose of a grade?

A Penny for Their Thoughts:

Chapter 7

Redos and retakes, really?

"You can't do retakes; they won't have redos in the real world."

Katelynn's Thoughts:

This is one of the most common arguments I hear about allowing for reassessment in our classrooms. And honestly, I don't think it's valid. At all. First of all, I address the problematic use of the phrasing "real world" with students in section 9. It is diminishing and detrimental to growth.

So you might then say, "Fine, if reassessment isn't 'real world,' retakes certainly won't prepare them for their futures." Again, I disagree.

In any job, commitment, or obligation, we are expected to do things well. Correctly, even. And when we don't, it is usually our responsibility to learn from our mistakes and fix them. We preach this to children all the time. "Learn from your mistakes" is such a common phrase that kids hear, I'm surprised we don't make the connection to reassessment.

In reassessment, we are advocating for our students to literally go back and fix their mistakes after they learn more. We are pushing them to achieve a better, deeper understanding and demonstrate their ability at a higher level. It is our expectation that they learn the material, master the skills, and become better humans in our classrooms.

So why in the world would we stop them from doing so by not allowing them to retake an assessment?

Retakes provide our students with tangible opportunities to demonstrate their progress and their growth. It gives students room to continue learning, and then shows us when they've come further in their journey. I absolutely want my students to continue progressing in my classroom past the assessment, especially if they didn't achieve their fullest potential the first time around.

If you truly want students to focus on learning, if you truly want them to feel less anxious about assessment, if you truly want to gather multiple points of data to demonstrate proficiency... Let. Them. Retake. The Assessment.

A lack of accountability is also cited as a reason to avoid redos in the classroom. But I actually believe the opposite—reassessment *promotes* accountability in our students. While many believe that students won't take the first assessment seriously, this is more about our approach to assessment as a whole. We have to help our students see assessment as a place for them to demonstrate their proficiency. They should be fully aware of the skill they are showing, and should see the assessment as a way to show us their understanding of that skill. In this environment, retakes aren't a crutch they rely on. Rather, students see them as a continuous ability to grow and demonstrate that growth to us. This is especially true for those students who might take a little longer to understand.

Moreover, at their heart, retakes are an accountability *measure*. It's literally in the design. Didn't master the material the first time? Well, I expect you to have these skills, so let's continue learning. Students are held accountable, in the truest sense of the word, to actually *meet* our learning goals. Doing poorly isn't a way out. It's not the end.

There are also plenty of structures that require our students to show accountability in reassessments. I know many teachers who have a retake form or contract, which requires students to acknowledge their previous level of understanding and speak to the new learning they have done. This not only promotes accountability, but also reflection.

Our goal in our classes is to help our students master material. If that is the case, we should honor the fact that some will take longer than others.

And we should provide them with the opportunities to showcase their growth and mastery, even after the initial assessment. I would argue that reassessment is a necessary component to all of our classes as we attempt to prepare our students for their futures. After all, if our content is so vital for them to master, we should expect them to actually do it.

Dave's Thoughts:

I love to run, but not because I am fast. As a matter of fact, most of you reading this could beat me in a 100-yard dash, but similarly, I could probably beat most of you in a marathon. So who is a better runner, you or me?

I drive a Nissan Sentra. It tops off at a maximum speed of about 90 m.p.h....don't ask me how I know. Just down the street, one of my neighbors drives a Porsche 911 with an estimated top speed of about 150 m.p.h. My car gets close to 45 miles to the gallon for gas consumption. My neighbor's car gets about 21 miles per gallon. His car is faster, but my car was cheaper to purchase and to operate. Does the speed of his car make it better?

Sometimes in life, speed matters. If you get rushed into the emergency room, getting a quick assessment could save your life. If you are an Uber driver or a taxi operator, time is literally money. If you work on a construction site, the longer a job takes you to complete, the fewer jobs you get to start. So yes, speed does matter, but...does it always?

As a father of four kids, I have read dozens of fables and short stories to my children in an attempt to both instill a love of reading and to teach some of life's truths. One of my all-time favorites is a story I am sure we are all familiar with, *The Tortoise and the Hare.* In this classic, we learn the valuable lesson that "slow and steady wins the race." We use this story to remind our children not to rush, to take their time, to have persistence, and that it will eventually be rewarded.

As a father, I use this story as an illustration when encouraging my children not to give up on routine skills like learning to play chess, tie their shoes, and learning to ride their bikes. Speed isn't important. Sticking with it and eventually learning is. I use this illustration when asking my children to slow down at the dinner table and just enjoy their food. I use this illustration in the classroom when students attempt to just rush through their work in an attempt to just get done without focusing on excellence. I use this at home when my children attempt to just get their homework done as quickly as possible so they can go outside and play without fully embracing the process of learning while doing their required assignments. I use this at practice when athletes attempt to plow through a drill or a stretch to just get it over with instead of paying close attention to their form and technique.

But then...as a classroom teacher, working to ensure my students are learning in the most effective and efficient way possible, I look at my pacing guide and realize I am behind where I am supposed to be, so I pick up the pace, skipping over superfluous information.

Then I require my students to complete their weekly Friday quiz because, well, it's the end of the week and they should all get it by now.

Then I start the timer for five minutes and tell my students to complete their timed fluency task because five minutes should be enough.

Then my juniors walk into the auditorium to begin taking the SAT. The time is set and students begin rushing through the assessment to answer as many questions as possible before they are forced to start filling in random guesses before the deadline hits them and the alarm warns them to put their pencils down.

Here's the truth:

I am in my mid-forties and am just now learning what it means to be humble, to be kind, to be forgiving, and to be forgiven. Many others learned these skills in their youth. I am glad my time is not up.

My oldest child is now sixteen. He learned to tie his shoes when he was ten. His younger brother was six when he learned how. I am glad they were given the time they each needed.

My daughter learned to walk at ten-months old. Her youngest brother learned to walk when he was fourteen-months old. I am so glad they each had the time they needed.

I ran my first marathon in 3 hours and 53 minutes. After ten years of training, I finished my most recent marathon in 4 hours 32 minutes. I am so glad I kept going even once my initial time goal elapsed.

Sometimes in life, speed matters. But when it comes to learning, slow and steady wins the race. One of the reasons we don't see the needle moving in schools today is because we get so focused on covering it all, in the time we have, that we sacrifice the process for the moment. We emphasize the pace over the product. We worry about breadth over depth, and this is where we keep missing the mark. Our instruction is a mile wide and an inch deep, when really, it should be just the opposite.

Sure, time is not unlimited, but neither is learning. Just as time marches on, so does our understanding. Learning is not a *got it* or *don't got it* dichotomy. Treating it as such only causes us to race even more. When we embrace the idea that learning is all about endurance, that understanding grows and develops eternally, then we can get ourselves more comfortable accepting that speed may not be all that it is cracked up to be.

~

Redos and retakes, really?

A Penny for My Thoughts:

65

Redos and retakes, really?

 **A Penny for Their Thoughts:**

Chapter 8

Should we assign homework?

Katelynn's Thoughts:

The past few years, this topic has undergone a barrage of scrutiny. From the arguments of it being absolutely necessary for a student's development, to the ones reviewing the number of hours students spend at school each day, it's a hotly contested issue. Then there's the consideration of including it in an overall grade, or if it has a place there at all. It's a pretty philosophical discussion, and one that should spark some reflection on practice.

What I can tell you is that getting rid of homework in my own classroom was one of the most positive decisions I made for student learning and student equity. There are still times when my students have to complete a class assignment that they did not finish during our block, or times when they've had work to do at home because of restrictions during our day. But for the most part, our class has no homework assignments that are handed to them with the expectation that they are completed independently, outside of school hours.

There are some instances where homework is warranted and necessary for students to develop an academic skill. There are times when it can be beneficial. However, I find that this is not true in a majority of situations. Most often, the work tends to be an extension of classwork that was already completed. Now, if a student was struggling and needed to practice further, that's one thing. But for students who are already understanding, who have already done the work to demonstrate that skill, homework just doesn't seem to have a legitimate purpose. If it's to keep things equal, I'll default to the notion that our classrooms should absolutely be fair, but definitely not equal.

I often hear teachers cite the need for homework because students need "practice." I see that argument being valid, though I don't understand the need for practice to involve repeating the same process 25 times. When a student has achieved proficiency at a skill, they don't particularly need the practice. Repeating that practice, however many times, isn't going to enhance their proficiency at the skill. What does enhance their proficiency is providing them with opportunities to extend and explore their understanding, especially if those opportunities challenge them to think beyond the classroom walls. For the students who *do* need practice because they have not yet mastered a skill, who's to say they can do this practice effectively on their own? If they do it incorrectly, they've just repeated the incorrect process over and over again, achieving nothing beneficial. If they copy the same correct process 25 times, they haven't developed a deeper understanding at all, but just gone through the motions of repetition, again achieving nothing beneficial.

On top of that, do we really need to hold kids 'accountable' by grading it? In my mind, if I cannot justify the homework assignment as advantageous for my students' learning, then why are they even doing it? If I cannot explain to my students the purpose behind their doing homework and my only course of action to get them to do it is to tell them it's for a grade, then is it really a necessary learning activity? My guess is no.

Homework should be an exercise that is low-stakes, furthering the notion that it's okay not to know something right away. It's okay not to understand, as long as you are trying to learn and seeking help. When we grade it and that grade negatively impacts a student, a few different things can happen. First, the students who don't understand the content see no value in doing it. It will only hurt them if they try and fail, shutting them down to the class, to you, and to putting forth the effort to learn. Second, the students who do get it are spending time on something they already know, just to get points. And we all know how I feel about points.

This does not mean that I think homework should not be assessed. It absolutely should. Students cannot learn from their mistakes if they don't know what those mistakes are. But there is a big difference between assessing and grading. Assessing work is focused on giving feedback to promote growth. The feedback should be focused on growth and should give students direction for how to move forward. I like to use a 3-part method:

1. Where is your learning? Use common language or a proficiency scale.
2. Why is it there? Specific reference to the student's work.
3. What are the next steps? How can they move to the next level of proficiency?

This feedback should not be used to penalize them once they master the skill. Their overall grade should communicate what they know now, not how many difficult attempts they had along the way. Students should not be in situations where they have shown their proficiency, but their academic grade (you know, the thing that's supposed to communicate how well they understand the content) should NOT suffer because they didn't understand it during practice.

Homework may have a place in education. But the antiquated practices that are still lingering must be revisited. We need to reflect on why we assign homework, what its purpose is, and who it's truly for. We need to take a look at our practices and procedures surrounding it, reconsider our why, and ensure that we are working for the good of our kids and their development. The reason for homework is shifting, its role is being redefined, and that is going to require some change. Wherever you stand on the issue, whichever camp you are in, this change is intimidating. Reflection on a deeply held belief or philosophy is always tough. But doing it will make you better. It will affect your students. It will change you.

So do your homework, and make sure you get it done. Your students are depending on you.

~

Dave's Thoughts:

Ready to read some ambiguity? Yes, I think you should assign homework, but I do not think you should ever use it for accountability or evidence collection purposes. Homework has value, but more importantly, it also has huge opportunity costs. Homework may help some students practice necessary and important skills, but it can also cause unnecessary trauma, stress, and family conflict. Giving students an hour of homework every night while we complain about a one hour staff meeting once a month seems a little hypocritical, but I guess that's not comparing apples to apples is it? I mean one has the opportunity for collaboration, dialogue, brainstorming, and celebration and the other is...homework.

Now, don't get me wrong. I think students should have opportunities for independent practice; I just don't think it should be required. Back when I coached basketball, after every practice I would suggest some drills my students should work on in their driveways, at neighborhood parks, or in their bedrooms. The idea was that the drills would manifest at the next practice and in the next game through improved performance. The games and the scheduled practices (classes) were where I would assess progress and determine next steps. I was a believer that the drills were valuable and would help. I would never suggest a time wasting activity simply because my athletes needed to have things to do every night. If I couldn't think of something to truly help them improve, nothing was assigned. If athletes chose not to do the work or had conflicts with time at home and with their families, I trusted them that they made a decision that was best for them in coordination with their parents. Sometimes we all get too busy to do the things we want to do.

But, students will never do homework unless it is a part of their grade, right? Wrong. Remember that saying, "Once you learn how to ride a bike, you never forget." Kids can learn the skill of bike riding when they are five-years old and continue to show mastery of this skill for decades, yet in our classrooms, we attempt to teach students a skill on Monday that is forgotten by Friday. When was the last time that you saw a child outside doing his "bike riding homework"? Truthfully, we see it all the time. Granted, kids aren't expected to complete a worksheet by labeling all of the parts of a bike. They are not told to practice their riding fluency by completing three laps around the block in a designated time requirement. But they are often seen outside practicing while they play. In many circumstances, they are actually working on complex skills that surpass ours. They may be able to hop curbs, ride with no hands, or skid through the local dirt track. When kids practice, they get better. When kids are having fun, they are willing to practice.

So, yes, feel free to assign homework, but also understand that you are the teacher. You are the one who is asked to help kids grow. You are the one with the responsibility to model grace. You are the one who is challenged with learning what inspires, what ignites, and what will make learning fun, whether at home or your classroom, because that is the learning that lasts.

A Penny for My Thoughts:

A Penny for Their Thoughts:

Chapter 9

Does competition and competitive scoring belong in the classroom?

Katelynn's Thoughts:

I'm an incredibly competitive person. I grew up athletic, involved in many team and individual sports, which only fed my competitive spirit. And another area that I viewed as a competition was grades.

My preoccupation with class ranking, GPA, and earning points was prevalent all throughout my education. In high school and college, I was obsessed with how I measured up to my peers. Conversations revolved around our scores on projects, papers, and exams. I remember discussing GPA boosting courses and which teachers were easy graders—all with the hope of finding the route to the A.

I spent a large portion of my educational experience focused on competing. I wanted to win. I wanted the highest GPA, the top class ranking, and all the accolades that came along with it. Looking back though, I'm amazed at how much this competition took away from me. Because in many cases, I'm not entirely sure what I learned. Competition is bred in our educational system, most notably through grades and points. Reflecting on my experiences, I can see very clearly that I viewed learning as a competition—as something to win or to lose. Because if it wasn't about winning or losing, then why was there a scoreboard?

Consider the metaphor of athletic competition. What would happen if we turned off the scoreboard? What would our driving factors be? Why would we play? It would be like practice. In practice there are no scoreboards. We are not there to compete. We are not there to see who is the best and worst. Our purpose is not to win. We are there to grow our skills. We are there to learn.

Then what, exactly, is the purpose of grading with points and percentages? When we assign points to assignments, we are encouraging competition among our students. We are encouraging them to quantify their learning and gauge themselves against each other.

It's easy to say that this is not the highlight of your grading practice and that you tell students to keep their percentages and scores to themselves. This was exactly my argument three years ago. But the fact of the matter is this: Your students are 100% talking about and comparing their grades. They are 100% competing with each other.

Quantifying a student's learning process is not a productive practice. It reduces their learning to a single letter, one that will either be a point of pride or shame. That quantity will be a source of pride only if it is the best compared to others and a source of shame if it is lower than the rest. By definition, grades promote comparison and, because it is our nature, a desire to come out on top.

Learning should be like practice. Our students' focus should be on growing their skill sets and mastering new things, whether it be a jump shot or an effective thesis statement. They should be working to improve their understanding and willing to try (and fail) at something new. They should be getting feedback that is designed to help them grow.

Learning should not be held to a standardized measuring stick. It should not consistently empower certain students and silence others. It should not encourage those who get there faster, while crushing those who need more guidance and time.

Learning should be an individual evolution. It should be a process that adapts and expands in each of our students. It should encourage them to persevere, to think, and to thrive. It's time to turn off the scoreboard. Because learning is not a competition.

Dave's Thoughts:

329 lbs. That is the image that was posted on Instagram this week by a friend of mine while standing on a scale in his bathroom. To many, they would see this number and question the health of my friend. Three hundred twenty-nine pounds is one hundred fifty pounds more than I weigh. Why would anyone take pride in sharing this picture with the world and celebrating this weight with so many others...well...a person who has spent the last eighteen months losing more than two hundred pounds. That's who. 329 lbs is an AMAZING celebration. 329 lbs represents months of hard work and sacrifice. 329 lbs is a testimony to what is possible with focus and effort.

I weigh one hundred eighty pounds. I run, on average, fifty miles per week. I compete in marathons. I am forty-four years old. I have a resting heart rate of sixty-one beats per minute. I visit the gym to lift weights five days a week. To many I would be an example of health. However, what if I also told you that I never met my grandfather on my dad's side because he died of a massive heart attack when my dad was still a teenager? What if I also told you that my dad had his first heart attack when he was in his 40's? What if I told you depression and diabetes were conditions that were prevalent on the maternal side of my family? Does your impression of my health change at all?

We are at an interesting time in American schools where numbers are used to try to tell stories, and often are used to try and tell the whole story. The reality is that numbers often represent a snapshot in time and without greater context, often tell us very little. I am a proponent for assessment. I believe in the power of formative assessment to help guide instruction. I believe teachers should work to become data literate, but this means helping them understand the full story behind data. Just as literacy in most schools is a focus on teaching students to make sense of letters and words

—teaching them to piece them together to make greater sense when used in full context—we all need to be data literate, able to understand that numbers in isolation rarely tell the full story and never show the future.

Take a look at the chart below. It represents real data based on real numbers. What it shows is that in my home state of Michigan, researchers have discovered a correlation. They have discovered that when kids are eating more ice cream, there are more childhood deaths associated with drowning. Again, this is a real statistic. Some may see this and come to the conclusion that ice cream should be banned. That it is causing the death of children. Others, however, may look a little deeper and begin to ask the right questions: When are kids eating ice cream? When are kids swimming? When they realize that both of these events occur more frequently in the summer, they may begin to realize that although ice cream consumption and drownings are correlated, they are not causes. Data, numbers, can tell us something, but rarely do they tell us everything.

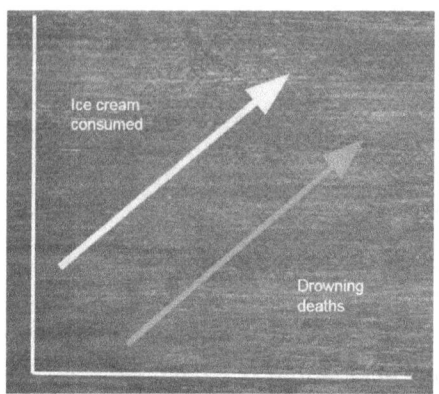

Earning a GPA of a 4.0 is an amazing accomplishment, but so is earning a 2.8 by a student who may have come from a home with no former high school graduates and little parental supervision.

Running a 3:45 marathon is incredible, but so is walking across the room for the first time in months, leaning on the shoulder of a hospice nurse after recovering from a life-altering stroke.

Giving a twelve-minute TED talk is fantastic, but so is listening to a child speak his first words as an infant learning to communicate.

We have to get ourselves to a place where we understand that numbers are important, but they NEVER tell us everything. Numbers guide toward the next question to ask, but should never be used as the answer. What numbers do you collect on kids...and adults...in your school? Do you know what they really say or have you already made up your mind?

Does competition and competitive scoring belong in the classroom?

A Penny for My Thoughts:

Does competition and competitive scoring belong in the classroom?

 **A Penny for Their Thoughts:**

Chapter 10

Rewards, trinkets, stickers, and clipcharts, really?

Katelynn's Thoughts:

Compliance is a component of classrooms that gets me fired up. Because the way classrooms were structured when I was a student, and the way many are structured now, is to enforce compliant students who do what they are told. Often, adults expect children to behave in ways we would not expect for ourselves. We want 100% on task behavior, a perfect record for turning in assignments on time, never an emotional outburst, and more.

My question is this—when have you *ever* been that perfect?

Our students are human beings. Real people. And they are *children.* Why, exactly, do we have such unrealistic expectations for them? And how do we expect them to achieve these expectations consistently, especially when we are watching them under a microscope, constantly looking for them to mess up?

Clip charts and other forms of behavior trackers—namely those that are public—are demoralizing and dehumanizing. They cause public humiliation (in children) and damage classroom community and teacher-student relationships. The benefits of using them are few and far between, and I cannot tell you how vast the harm can be.

I am an adult woman, and I can still remember with perfect clarity the day my card got switched from green to yellow *in first grade*. I can still feel my six-year-old face heating up, my heartbeat racing, and my absolute shame at having yelled out during a lesson. Sitting in my chair, I vowed then and there to never talk in my first-grade class again. And I didn't. For the next four months, I did not say a word in my classroom for fear of further humiliation. My teacher called my parents to ask if there was something going on at home because my attitude in class had changed. I refused to explain to my parents why I had become a very different student for fear that they would be disappointed in my behavior.

This story is one that I'm sure many others can identify with because it was a common practice. Using forms of public shame were (and in some places, still are) a method of enforced compliance and behavior management.

I say this not to call anyone out, but to inspire reflection. Instead of focusing on enforcing behavior, consider how you might *teach* students ways of coping, responding, or engaging. Help them learn and grow, but also give them grace and understanding when they make mistakes. Because, like you, they will make mistakes. And they do not deserve to be humiliated for something that is so fundamentally human.

Furthermore, consider how you encourage or reinforce behavior. Extrinsic motivators can do more harm than good. Instead of bolstering the positive behaviors because they are *right*, these motivators reinforce the pursuit of that behavior for the thing they get. Rather than teaching our students to behave in a productive, helpful way because that is what they should do, we are teaching them to do it *for* something.

On top of that, we have to consider the biases of these rewarding systems and the groups of students that consistently fall outside of the desired behavior category. We have to reflect on the ways we may be perpetuating systemic racism or oppression, and how our reward or punishment systems might consistently deny some students access.

So I ask for reflection. When we use extrinsic motivators like rewards, prizes, and stickers, what are we rewarding students for? Who are we excluding? Are the same students being publicly praised, time and time again, while others are never being acknowledged? Do the systems you have in place enforce compliance or teach positive interaction? Are we harming relationships or helping our students thrive?

Instead of utilizing extrinsic motivators and rewards, focus on building community and relationships with students. Not just teacher-student relationships, but those among the students in your class as well. Set intentions or expectations for the year—together. Co-create a set of guidelines that everyone has a voice in and refer to them frequently, so they don't fall by the wayside as the year progresses. When students make a mistake, be curious. Talk with them about the motivation of that behavior and use it as an opportunity to bolster that connection and reinvigorate the classroom community. When inappropriate or disruptive behavior happens—because it does—respond from a place of compassion. Consequences for actions are fair and should happen, but should not be given to hurt or humiliate. The focus should be restorative, on developing strategies for future success and helping navigate the difficulty of the moment. And we should always instill in our students that we value them.

～

Dave's Thoughts:

Here is the reality: if my employer decided tomorrow to stop paying me, I would not show up for work the next day. I work to get paid and to support my family, but work does not consume my entire day. As a matter of fact, I work so that I can afford to pursue my passions and my interests. Learning, growing, and improving are some of those interests. I say this because, to be quite blunt, I am tired of people telling kids that school is their job. It's not. Kids cannot quit. Kids have no other options. Kids attend school to learn, to grow, and to explore. It is our job to make learning enjoyable, to encourage risk taking and innovation, and to inspire creativity. It is not our job to introduce students to an extrinsically motivated token economy.

Improving, learning, and growing are all rewarding. Kids love to improve. As a father of four kids, I can vividly remember the moments when my kids all realized they could spell their own names, when they rode their bikes for the first time, and when they read their first chapter books. My kids did not complete these tasks to earn a sticker, meaningless points, or even a few bucks from me. They did them because they wanted to feel a sense of accomplishment. They wanted to achieve. They were inspired intrinsically.

I have sometimes made the mistake of creating extrinsic drivers at home, however, and I pay the price...literally. My oldest child now argues if I ask him to mow the lawn without first offering him ten dollars to complete the chore. I have created a barter system where my kids expect donuts on Sunday mornings in exchange for their willing attendance at church. My children now see doing things for the family or their own growth as deserving of compensation instead of for the good of the task itself. Intrinsic motivation is lost. It will take conscious effort on my part to reverse the damage I have done, while trying to reestablish lifelong learning. Rewards may work in the short term, but will always come back to haunt us in the long run. Research supports this. Rewards work for incentivizing short-term goals but have an inverse effect on sustained efforts.

Clip charts fire me up on a whole new level. If you're not an elementary school teacher, you may not even be aware of what a clip chart is, but for those of you who teach in the K-5 world, you are probably all too familiar with these colorful monstrosities. Used as a means of publicly humiliating children in an attempt to curb unwanted behaviors, classrooms utilize these tools to try and manipulate childhood behavior. These rooms are often places where relational trauma exists at the expense of relationship building. Is that too blunt? Sorry, but our responsibility as educators is to provide an environment free of emotional harm, free from bullying and belittling. Attempting to coerce children into compliance or face public embarrassment is not only an ill-informed method of external motivation, but a form of public humiliation and shame as well. High schools, you are not immune. Public celebrations of honor roll, Top Ten lists, and other exclusionary practices aimed to sort and select and isolate those who may not play the game of school as we have designed it are no better. Let's start celebrating growth, celebrating progress, and celebrating mastery. Our celebrations are feedback. Feedback without the ability to improve is just judgment. When any of us feel judged, isolated and excluded, we don't necessarily feel the same level of commitment and investment to succeed as those put on the pedestal. But these are just my thoughts. I'll stop now before I offend everyone. What do you think?

Rewards, trinkets, stickers, and clipcharts, really?

A Penny for My Thoughts:

Rewards, trinkets, stickers, and clipcharts, really?

A Penny for Their Thoughts:

Part Three

Equity

[ek-wi-tee] something that is fair and just

— Dictionary.com

"Our calling is to drop our egos, commit to removing barriers, and treat our learners with the unequivocal respect and dignity they deserve."

— Mirko Chardin and Katie Novak — *Equity by Design*

"We cannot guarantee outcomes, but we can guarantee access."

— Cornelius Minor — *We Got This*

"Supreme Court to Revisit Race-Based College Admissions"

— US News and World Report. January 24, 2022

"Teachers, Parents File Lawsuit Against New Hampshire's 'Divisive Concepts' Law"

— US News and World Report. December 13, 2021

"Plans for free Pre-K and community college could provide a 'ladder into the middle class'"

— New York Times. July 16, 2021

"Parent-activists, seeking control over education, are taking over school boards"

— The Washington Post. January 19, 2022

"Lawsuit against Georgetown, other schools, renews questions over admissions practices"

— The Washington Post. January 16, 2022

Headlines like these abound daily in newspapers across the United States. Debates rage in school board meetings, in courtrooms, and in living rooms, but do they belong in the classroom?

Educators today are faced with increasing pressures to engage in social justice reform initiatives, to fight for access, and to ensure that we provide opportunities for each child and the families they represent. These conversations are happening and are on the mind of the nation, so it's inevitable that they will enter our schools. Does this mean we are expected to enter into these large and complex conversations? Or do we stick to the script and deliver the curriculum with our heads down? Do we bring the outside world into the classroom or do we leave it behind as we cross the threshold of our school building? Do we share our thoughts and feelings with our colleagues even if it means we may offend and divide? Do we participate in activism, marching, shouting, and sharing? Do we speak freely or risk looking like we are over sharing? Do we start the debate even if the debate hasn't entered our town? Do we expand our horizons so the world is always within our view?

As we explore the world of educational equity, we must remember these conversations take many different shapes and forms. Each of us enters these conversations from our own perspectives and with our own biases. We see the world through our own lens, as does everyone on the outside of our own consciousness. The debates will continue on the outside of our four walls. Consider for yourself whether you will choose to bring them inside.

Chapter 11

Does all really mean all?

Katelynn's Thoughts:

A popular sentiment in education is the belief that all kids can learn. I remember proudly writing that in all the applications for my first teaching job, thinking how great it sounded. But, like many buzzwords or phrases in education, the way it comes across is really the point. It *sounds* fantastic, so we share our stance, loudly and proudly for all to hear.

This particular idea, that **all** students can learn, is something we say, but I see a lot of actions that point to the contrary. Our wavering position comes through most commonly in the language we use to refer to certain groups of children.

When we use phrasing like "Title I Teacher" or "at-risk population" or "urban school," we are signaling something—and it isn't about the environment or location of the school. What we're indicating in this kind of language is that the children in these environments are different from others. There is a largely negative connotation associated with how this is presented. When we look at the demographics of these populations, it becomes deeply troubling. In Title I schools, over 15 million students are

Black or Hispanic, a reflection of the institutional racism and inequitable structures that exist in the system (Annie E. Casey Foundation, 2021). Our use of this language, this distinction, then starts to hit a little too close to white saviorism, or the idea that we, the largely white teaching profession, is somehow here to save the poor students in our classrooms. The subtext is that the population being served is somehow less—less smart, less capable, less compliant.

Not only does that perpetuate racism, but it isn't at all in line with our professed belief that all students can learn. If we truly believe that **all** students can learn, we have to live that truth and stop implying that certain groups learn less than others.

~

Dave's Thoughts:

I had the most incredible third-grade teacher ever. She knew me. She noticed me. She made me feel valued and she told me I was smart. As a matter of fact, she went a step further and told me I was gifted. She believed in me so much that at the end of my third-grade year, she convinced my parents to allow me to skip the fourth grade and jump right into fifth grade, where I would then become classmates with my older sister.

For the rest of my K-12 school experience, I was given the reputation as "the smart kid." I was made to believe that intelligence was simply something given to me at birth and that because of my very existence on earth, everything would always just come easy to me. I even had the label of "Gifted and Talented" next to my name in my teachers' grade books to prove it. Then, reality kicked in.

As we all already know, life, when being lived well, is not always easy. Things will be difficult. Things will stretch us and cause some growing pains. Unfortunately for me, this was a lesson that took forty-one years to uncover. From the time I received my gifted label as an elementary student until well into my adult years, I believed my responsibility was to continue to make everyone believe that everything was easy for me. I created facades of confidence. I shied away from risks and chances. I lived a life of blame and accusation any time things did not go according to my plans. I believed that it was up to me to live an easy life and that if anything was a struggle, it was not my fault. This was my existence until I finally hit rock bottom as a man more than forty years old, twenty years into his career, raising four kids. I found myself alone. I found myself facing rejection. I found myself confused and feeling completely isolated.

I was diagnosed with depression. I was prescribed medication and even found myself checked into a local hospital as a result of the dark thoughts I began to have.

You see, my reality was wrapped up in the label I received as an eight-year-old child. I believed that everything was supposed to come easy, because, well, my teacher told me so. She validated me and made me believe I was not like the other kids. I began to swell with confidence. I had a false arrogance. I shunned help and rejected others. It took me hitting rock bottom to realize that life is hard, for everyone. It took me hitting rock bottom to realize it is OK to struggle. It took me hitting rock bottom to realize that asking for help is not a sign of weakness, but a sign of strength.

Often in educational circles, we reject the concept of labeling kids as a result of their perceived deficiencies and struggles. We know the negative impact labels such as "at-risk" can have on a child, but I am here to warn against the use of all labels, even those we might perceive as positive. The truth is, kids will always live up to their labels. It is our job to help students live up to their identities. There is a huge difference. Knowing the difference between each child and every child is THE difference.

≈

Does all really mean all?

A Penny for My Thoughts:

Does all really mean all?

A Penny for Their Thoughts:

Chapter 12

Do families really matter? What role should families play in school?

Katelynn's Thoughts:

Every August, before students enter my class for the first time, I send a letter to their families. It is not a syllabus or a letter that outlines all my policies, nor does it really talk about our class and how it will run. It is a letter that thanks families for sharing their child with me for the year. That is its sole purpose—to share my gratitude for the beautiful opportunity I have to spend so much time with someone else's baby.

You see, it's a truly incredible thing we educators get to do each year. We welcome a fresh group of children into our classrooms, typically excited to show up for the next year. We get to spend huge chunks of the day with them, building relationships, creating a community, getting to know them, seeing them grow and change, and helping them through the discovery of their identity.

And those kids belong to somebody. They are the light of someone's life, someone's pride and joy. Their families send them, the loves of their life, to us. During the school year, they spend more hours with us than at home. They go through some of the most difficult and the most rewarding experiences of their childhoods and teenage years in our schools. We get to see all of it. We get to bear witness to their evolution, often influencing it ourselves.

When I take the time to think about it, I am so amazed by all the beauty we get to witness with our kids. And I am so incredibly thankful that their families trust me to be a part of their child's life. That they send their child to me, so I might help them grow, evolve, and *become*. So I send a letter. To express my gratefulness that I have such a wildly beautiful opportunity and let families know that their influence and their input absolutely does matter.

~

Dave's Thoughts:

"Don't worry, parents. We got this."

"It's like pulling teeth to get parents to show up."

I have made both statements as an educator and have heard both of these as a parent. In schools, we are notorious for playing the blame game. Colleges blame high schools. High schools blame middle schools. Middle schools blame elementary schools and elementary schools blame parents. While most of the blame game is played in an attempt to release us from responsibility, what we are also inadvertently doing is attributing an impact factor. When we say, "Last year's teacher could have done more," we are also acknowledging the impact last year's teacher had. Similarly, when we blame parents for a student's misbehavior or lack of responsibility, we are staking a claim in the power of parents to influence their children.

I am here to say emphatically that I believe parents matter and it is our responsibility to make sure they recognize it, but far too often, our hypocritical behaviors do more to push parents away than we even realize.

We tell parents that we value family time and then send kids home with homework that causes stress, arguments, and bitterness.

We tell parents that we want them to create memories with their children and to be active in the lives of their kids, but then chastise the child who comes to us to say she will be missing a few days of school to go on a family vacation.

We call parents in the middle of the day on their office lines to complain about their child's behavior, but we don't reply to a confused e-mail sent at 6pm because it is *our time.*

We tell parents that "we got this" and "we are the professionals" and then get upset when parents don't volunteer to support or show up for conferences.

The reality is, we must always assume the good and doubt the bad. We must believe that all parents are really doing the best they can and that all kids are good kids. As teachers, it is our responsibility to teach adults just as much as it is our responsibility to teach children. As a matter of fact, the best way to teach children is to teach their parents. If we are willing to acknowledge the negative impact a parent can have on a child, we must also acknowledge the positive impact. We know that the apple rarely falls far from the tree, so let's start tending to the trees a little more and watch the quality of the fruit improve.

Parent-teacher conferences should not be used to simply explain a report card grade (see my rant on the purpose of grading). This is an opportunity for both the parent and the teacher to learn more so that each can do more. This is an opportunity to connect and share, to collaborate and to each lean into the unique relationship the other has with the child. As educators we are always looking for ways to have a bigger impact on our students. We can spend hours at home on Teacher Pay Teacher and Pinterest looking for the next best trick and gimmick, or we can spend the same amount of time on the phone, on our e-mail, or on social media (using whatever tool possible) to connect with those who have proven to have an impact on our students, their parents. Yes, parents matter.

What role should families play in school?

A Penny for My Thoughts:

What role should families play in school?

A Penny for Their Thoughts:

Chapter 13

Who has the power?

Katelynn's Thoughts:

Power shows up in every organization. The structure of power, no matter what form it takes, is a point of contention in many circles. When we consider what is equated with power, it's often influence and control of others.

In classrooms, there existed an air of authority that exists between teacher and student. Traditionally, teachers held the power over students and mandated compliance, quiet, and a strict adherence to rules. Often, these policies unfairly targeted students of color, forcing assimilation or doling out consequences in a biased manner.

The remnants of this power structure still exist. Consider the rules that require students to ask to use the restroom, trade their shoe for a pencil, or stay seated and quiet unless called upon. Remember the teacher who enforced compliance through embarrassment and calling students out. Imagine the powerlessness felt by students as they sat in their seats, silently waiting to be told what to do.

This power dynamic harms children, and it is not conducive to their learning and development. When we consider what it means to be a leader, which teachers absolutely are, in my mind there is one quality that all leaders share. *They empower others.*

When we empower students in our classrooms, we communicate an important message: that they are valued. We shift the dynamic from one of compliance to one of exploration, failure, and growth. Our students are left feeling supported, confident, and ready to take on the challenges set before them. They take an active role in their learning and in their education, and the act of ownership begins to take hold.

On the other hand, if we continue to hold on to power for ourselves, we maintain control while sacrificing student progress. We diminish our students' roles to that of a consumer, standing idly by in their education. Risk taking is discouraged, as students must follow the rules at all costs. They are no longer owning their learning. Instead, it is something happening *to* them.

The classroom power dynamic becomes even more concerning when we consider the demographics of educators. The profession itself is 79% white. Only 7% of educators are Black, 9% are Latinx, and 1% are Indigenous, Asian, or multiracial (National Center for Education Statistics, 2019). The notion that a largely White profession has traditionally and continues to exercise power and control over a student body that includes far more students of color is a problem. It reinforces to students, especially BIPOC students, the notion of white supremacy and assimilation.

This issue is even further compounded when we consider school leaders, such as principals and superintendents. As a whole, teachers are 24% male, but principals are 46% male. While the percentage of male principals is dropping, it is still troubling that nearly half of principals are male. With superintendents, only 27% are female. The trouble is that in a female-dominated profession, the majority of leadership is male. This issue doesn't just end with gender. A female principal or superintendent might be uncommon, but BIPOC are largely underrepresented in educational leadership. 22% of principals and 8.6% of superintendents identify as BIPOC (National Center for Education Statistics, 2019). Even if data is not your area of expertise, it's abundantly clear that there is a problem.

Consider who has the power in our schools and in our classrooms. Address the biases that exist within you. The internal belief that leaders must be strong, tough, and logical is simply code for male. Our idea that quiet and compliance is equivalent to respect is false. The belief that care and nurturing tendencies can only be feminine is wildly untrue. The notion that assimilation is the key to success is not only wrong; it is racist. We must work to dismantle the power structures that exist to benefit certain small groups of people and ensure that our students do the same.

Dave's Thoughts:

In the United States today, 76% of all teachers are female, yet only 54% of principals are female, and only 27% of superintendents are female (National Center for Education Statistics). As a man, I see the issue here. I know for a fact that I have been the recipient of tremendous amounts of privilege and opportunity at the expense of others. I also recognize, that although I have been afforded the nice titles and the comfortable offices, that I am not necessarily the one with the most influence.

Influence has nothing to do with a placard or a title. I know this because at home I am known as "dad" and quite often I am simply at the whim of everyone else in the household. My title carries with it very little influence. Being outnumbered by my four kids, I know that a mutiny can happen at any time. At work, I have been a principal, a director, and a professor. I am an evaluator. I am a teacher. I have dozens of workplace tasks that define my role, but none of them define my power and influence. Five hundred students, sixty-five staff members, only one me. My title may give me some authority, but authority without influence matters little.

Too often in organizations, we see individuals who carry with them the title "boss" and erroneously believe that this also equates to influence. Often it is the boss who makes the biggest miscalculation. I absolutely believe that respect is given and not earned. I wholeheartedly believe that respect is a basic human right. That is not to say that respect, authority, and power all equate to influence. Influence and the power to change thoughts, actions, and beliefs very rarely come from positional authority.

I completely recognize that sometimes simply because of my title, my ability to influence is negated. I have had a big office. I have had a private phone line. I have degrees and have written books. I get to travel the country speaking and presenting, yet as much as I love all of this, at times all of this can actually get in the way of getting the job done if I allow it to. In an attempt to change mindsets and create enhanced culture, some may rebuff my ideas and suggestions simply because I am the boss and for no other reason. One thing that I have recognized is that often in schools, influence and pay have an inverse relationship. If you are a leader and you really want to change your school, don't try to do it alone. If you want the masses to buy in, convince your secretaries, custodians, and paraprofessionals first. They are often the toughest critics, your most vocal employees, and the ones with the greatest power to leverage your leadership. The real power does not come from those with the biggest paycheck. It comes from those with the biggest audience.

I have heard many administrators make the statement, "I do everything for the kids." This is an amazing mindset and one that I hold on to. This does not mean that in working with and for your students that you make the lives of the adults miserable. If you want to enhance the lives of your students, work to enhance the lives of those on the front lines. Only once a leader realizes his or her ability to lead depends more on those who follow, and his or her ability to serve them, will change begin taking root.

If you really want to see where the power and influence lies in any organization, get a hold of the payscale, turn it upside down, then start with the top. Real leaders understand that bold humility is what gets the job done.

~

A Penny for My Thoughts:

A Penny for Their Thoughts:

Chapter 14

Do kids need a dress code? (Do adults?)

Katelynn's Thoughts:

W hen it comes to a dress code, I immediately think of equity. Because when we look at the way school dress codes are traditionally written, they are written specifically and overwhelmingly for girls. Spaghetti straps, skirt length, midriff-baring... all terms traditionally found in dress codes, and all items that show up almost exclusively on girls' clothing.

I say girls here, rather than young women, on purpose. The children these dress codes traditionally target are girls—they are still kids, many of whom are dealing with a wide variety of personal struggles with identity and fitting in. And while it might seem that dress codes exist to fix that problem, they really, really don't.

When we begin policing girls' bodies, we are sending a strong subliminal message. Not just that their bodies are to be hidden away, but that they are objects of desire. The presence of their bodies is distracting, inappropriate, even wrong. Imagine being 12-years old and told that your body is unacceptable, that you need to cover it up, because you are "going to get a reputation." Damaging words to hear as a child. Ones that stick with you, and can leave a lasting impression.

On top of that, when a girl is caught violating the dress code, or dress coded, she's often put in one of two positions. She's either sent home from school, missing out on her own education to prioritize that of the boys she's supposedly distracting, or she's required to change into something absolutely humiliating, often chosen for that very reason. This is not just unfair; it's wrong. We are teaching girls that it is their responsibility to cover themselves up, for fear of how others might react. We are teaching them that this modesty is more important than their learning. We are teaching them that their bodies and femininity are wrong and inappropriate, and should be hidden. They are learning, from us, that if they dress a certain way, they are, in fact, asking for it.

And when we consider young Black girls? The discrepancy becomes even more appalling. In a 2018 report done by the National Women's Law Center, it was found that Black girls were 20.8% more likely than white girls to be apprehended for dress code violations. Not only does this indicate that we value the education of Black girls less than the boys, but we also value it even less than their white counterparts at school.

When all of this is considered, the issue of a dress code becomes about sexism, racism, and gender bias. Which are all things our schools should be actively working to dismantle, rather than perpetuate.

That does not mean, however, that we do not need to teach our girls about modesty and valuing their bodies. We absolutely *must* be teaching these things, especially with the rise of social media. What we need to avoid, though, is policing their bodies in such a way that reinforces the opposite. Consequences for some girls but not others, inadvertently (or deliberately) regulating Black girls over white girls, including biased violations like head wraps or religious garments—these do not teach girls that they are valuable and worthy of an education. Instead, they enforce racialized gender biases, prioritize learning of certain groups of children over others, and humiliate our students into submission.

And that just isn't okay. When we write our dress codes (if we truly need them), they should be focused on equitable language that centers the children—the human beings—in our schools. It should include the input of those for those whom we are writing them for, to ensure that they are being represented fairly and inclusively. It should ensure that students are able to feel safe, comfortable, and respected in school. And when it comes to enforcing dress codes, we absolutely have to check our own biases and privilege to ensure that we are promoting the growth of every single one of the students in our care.

~

Dave's Thoughts:

OK, time to ride the fence. Dress code sounds kind of harsh and rigid. Do kids sometimes need guidance and suggestion? Yes. Do kids deserve to be placed in a box removed of freedom of expression and personal identity? No.

This is going to sound a lot like hyperbole, but I believe some of you will be able to see the connection. Two years ago I began going to counseling and seeking support. I was diagnosed with depression and anxiety. I was placed on medication and had scheduled meetings with a therapist each week. For the last two decades, since I became an adult and a professional, I have lived a life trying to be the person everyone else wanted me to be. I lived my life in a facade, more worried about fitting in than standing out. I was so nervous about not winning the approval of society that after twenty years as an adult, forty years on earth, I lost sight of who I was and what my personal passions were.

I don't want you to read this and infer that I believe a dress code will create students who are clinically depressed and anxious, but I do believe that often in schools we find ourselves more focused on teaching children how to blend in and how to conform to the masses than we do allowing children to celebrate who they are and who they were created to become.

We should encourage children to embrace their uniqueness. We should celebrate them for getting a mohawk or a perm. We should embrace it when they grow a mullet or an afro. Similarly, we should allow them to wear a hoodie or a tank top. We should allow them to wear a shirt displaying a love for their favorite sport's team or movie. Kids should be allowed to be kids, but more importantly, they should be allowed to be themselves.

I also understand that sometimes dress codes are put in place to try and level the playing field. In some schools, dress codes exist to "protect" students by working to eliminate the perception of the haves from the have nots. As a person who did not have his first pair of name brand shoes until college, I get it. I noticed the Jordans others were wearing and I was all too aware of the K-Mart brand shoes I was wearing. I know this contributed to some of my insecurities and struggles, but at the same time, I also was given opportunities to continue to be me in other ways. My parents encouraged me to embrace our struggles and to be the best I could be. As much as I wished I could have had what others had, pursuing the masses for the sake of keeping up with the others, would have had a negative impact on my individualism as well. As you work on creating policies for kids, I know you have the best interests of every kid in mind, but more importantly, focus on each kid.

Oh, and the same is true for you...jeans, hoodies, and tennis shoes to work? Yes, please...but please leave the yoga pants at home...or maybe I am being a sexist hypocrite :)

～

Do kids need a dress code? (Do adults?)

A Penny for My Thoughts:

Do kids need a dress code? (Do adults?)

A Penny for Their Thoughts:

Part Four

Student Voice

[vois] the right to present and receive consideration of one's desires or opinions

— Dictionary.com

In education, student voice refers to the values, opinions, beliefs, perspectives, and cultural backgrounds of individual students and groups of students in a school, and to instructional approaches and techniques that are based on student choices, interests, passions, and ambitions.

— https://www.edglossary.org/student-voice/

Students who believe they have a voice in school are seven times more likely to be academically motivated than students who do not believe they have a voice.

— Quaglia Institute for School Voice and Aspirations,
2016

Transforming a school into one that values and maintains strong student voice is seldom accomplished without facing hurdles that can dilute or derail efforts. Building a culture of voice can be challenged by the various implicit definitions found in educational and lay circles. The inability to articulate what student voice is and what it looks like has allowed school and student leaders alike to form definitions suited to their preferences and agendas, thereby limiting the scope and effectiveness of efforts to create a culture that values and promotes authentic student voice.

— National Student Council-Raising Student Voice and
Participation Executive Summary

It's Not Ours to Give–Katelynn's story

Aaron was an energetic eleven-year old who bounded into middle school like a golden retriever. He was excited, eager, and outgoing. He made friends quickly and was incredibly silly, but in the most endearing way. But Aaron's real gift was his imagination. He had incredible ideas, ones that he loved to share, and they were brilliant in their uniqueness.

In the first week of school, I ask my students to write about writing. I ask them to take some time to tell me specifically about themselves as writers—who they are, what their experience has been like, what works for them, what doesn't. They are quick to ask me if they can talk about how much they dislike it, and I always respond that I WANT to hear about that. And I mean it.

Aaron took this job very seriously. He dove into the task, furiously writing on his looseleaf paper. He didn't look up or drop his pencil until the end of the period, and even then, I'm not sure if he was done. When I went to review the responses, I shuffled through each of them, skimming their thoughts and ideas. Many were expected, some were surprising, and some were lackluster. But then, I saw Aaron's.

His paragraph started with the line, "What I hate about writing is how there is so much freedom taken away." He went on to describe all the typical writing he'd been asked to do—about his summer and bats and waterparks—and how it took all the fun and imagination out of it. Instead, he wanted to write about "intergalactic wars, dastardly pirates pillaging and plundering, and superheroes destroying supervillain's dreams." I was struck. The vocabulary and sentence structure, sure. But the clear desire to communicate and express ideas was what hit me hardest. And I couldn't help but wonder... what if I never allowed this voice, HIS voice, to come through? I would never have seen this beauty, this potential, had I not just sat back and let him flow.

So now, when I consider student voice in the classroom, I'm careful to remember Aaron. He didn't need me to give him his voice—none of them do. They just need us to give them the space, the freedom, to use it.

When you think of student voice, what words do you use?

When we talk about student voices, I have a hard time not getting into the colloquialism of how we refer to it. Many people, myself included, like to assert that we need to give our students a voice. And while I understand the sentiment, I have a hard time with the phrasing. Because each time I hear it, I'm reminded of Aaron on his first week in my Language Arts classroom.

Chapter 15

Do kids need recipes for success (five paragraph essays and algorithms)?

Katelynn's Thoughts:

N o. Honestly I could leave it at that, but for you, dear reader, I'll elaborate. And because writing and language are my background, I'll start first with the five-paragraph essay.

Consider a piece of writing that has influenced you, changed your perspective, or left a lasting impression on your life. Was that piece structured in five paragraphs with an introduction, three supporting body paragraphs, and a conclusion? I doubt it. We want our students to grow into writers, and to do this, we must provide them with organizational skills. This should not be boxed and packaged into five neat paragraphs, each following the same basic outline. We should teach them to gather their ideas, consider their audience, and utilize a structure that best communicates their idea. Because that's what *writers* do. They communicate through written expression, compose beautiful prose that aims to entertain, inform, or persuade. They take readers on a journey in their pages through their beliefs, their stories, or their research. *People who write*, on the other hand, follow a prescribed formula that generates a robotic, cookie-cutter response. There is no enjoyment, no true author's purpose, because there is no author. There's just a student filling in the blanks.

And before you agree with me on writing, let me also make this plain. When we provide our students with a plug it in mode of learning, whether that be an algorithm, a formula, or anything else, we are not encouraging learning. Learning is to explore,

inquire, and discover. And while concepts like algorithms do exist, they first began as theories. As ideas or explorations, waiting to be defined. Why, then, would we not encourage our students to explore them? To rediscover the algorithm as it stands? To fully understand its origins because they themselves worked through its discovery? Proofs, you say? Don't wait until sophomore geometry to begin this practice. Encourage questions and challenges—and provide the time for learning.

Dave's Thoughts:

If you are reading this, odds are, like me, you live in a new world of education, a temporary world, but a world that is creating opportunities for amazing conversations that can lead to lasting changes and lasting learning.

We are asking each other questions like:

- How do we decide what is most important to teach?
- How do we determine what to grade and what a grade means?
- How do we balance making connections with making curriculum meaningful?
- In essence, how do we make learning last?

Asking these questions allows us a powerful opportunity to change our status quo and to begin focusing on the things that matter most. We have the chance to focus on the focus. We have the opportunity to examine why we do what we do and how we can focus on learning that lasts.

I've used this example before, but it is relevant here just as it was there. "Once you learn to ride your bike, you never forget." We have heard this saying countless times, and we all know it to be true. We can learn to ride a bike, a truly complex skill involving gross motor skills, fine motor skills, dexterity, balance, and coordination, by the time we are five-years old, and even without constant practice and study we are be able to hop back onto a bike decades later and still be able to ride. Why is that? I mean, some of us (professional educators) struggle to teach students in our classrooms, a skill on Monday that they will still remember five days later, yet children can go out onto the sidewalks of their neighborhood and learn an extremely complex skill that lasts a lifetime. Why?

Riding a bike is actually extremely complex. We cannot argue that we remember how to ride because it is easy to learn. Nor can we argue that we remember it because of its complexity. There are dozens of complex phenomena that I wish I understood better, but I just can't seem to grasp (how in the world do airplanes stay in the air...I mean, seriously). The reason we remember how to ride is because of how we learn, not what we are learning. The process we use to learn this skill is actually the same process we can use in our classrooms.

I spent a decade as a classroom teacher prior to becoming an administrator. When I was a teacher, I thought I was amazing. I thought my students were engaged, compliant, and respectful. The truth is, looking back on it now, although my students were great at playing school, I have real questions about whether I taught them anything that would have lasted beyond my classroom.

You see, the real reason kids are able to learn to ride their bikes isn't because of our ability to deliver high-quality content. It isn't because we are great speakers, have fancy PowerPoint presentations, or amazing rules and procedures. The only way to learn anything that lasts is to do. To stop sitting around thinking, copying, and pondering, and start doing. Lasting learning comes from doing.

I am the father of four children. I know emphatically that even though I read every parenting book I could find prior to the birth of my oldest child, I didn't really learn how to be a parent until I became a parent.

As a beginning teacher two decades ago, I know for a fact that when I entered my first classroom after four-and-a-half years of classes at the university level, I didn't really learn how to teach until I started teaching.

Lasting Learning comes from doing.

Right now you have an amazing opportunity to recognize this and to capitalize on it. We have an opportunity to focus learning on doing, not just hearing. We get the opportunity to have our students applying their knowledge. We get the opportunity to have our students fall down, skin their knees, and get back up. We get the chance to set small goals, to have our students get to the next driveway, then the next, before riding around the block. We get the chance to be cheerleaders running alongside our learners as they embrace new skills. We get the chance to get out of the way and let our kids go and watch them grow.

It is ironic that we give our students an F and a referral when they copy off of their peers but we give them an A when they copy our words and ideas. Let's let kids learn. Let's let kids do. Let's get out of the way and facilitate opportunities and let learning last a lifetime.

Do kids need recipes for success (five paragraph essays and algorithms)?

A Penny for My Thoughts:

Do kids need recipes for success (five paragraph essays and algorithms)?

A Penny for Their Thoughts:

Chapter 16

Why do students deserve voice and choice?

Katelynn's Thoughts:

As we consider this question, it's important to think critically about what is truly being asked. The students we serve are human beings, and they exist in our classrooms a sum of their humanity. Their voices and choices are things to be valued in the learning environment, and they most certainly deserve to use them fully.

When we dig a little deeper into this question, it is asking us to consider how we might personalize the learning of our students. And that is a poignant question. Because when we think of the uniqueness of each of our students, the varied nature of their voice, the undoubtedly wide range of their choices—it can seem overwhelming to allow for the full breadth of those possibilities.

But we must. Not only because they are human beings who deserve it, but also because we have a special opportunity to provide our students with a safe space to discover, fail, learn, and grow. Because when we do, their education becomes *theirs*.

Now, this is important. If you are looking for research or the backing to implement this approach, this is where you begin. Ownership over their learning is powerful for many reasons, but one that sticks out most to me is that it builds intrinsic motivation. Intrinsic motivation is the gold standard in education. What if we could get students to *want to learn?* What if we could get them to buy in? What if we could increase engagement? Well, we can. And it's simpler than we might think.

The self-determination theory of motivation (Ryan & Deci, 2000) tells us that intrinsic motivation increases when three basic needs are met: competency, autonomy, and relatedness. Competency refers to the perception of being **able** to do something, relatedness refers to how we make content **relevant,** and autonomy refers to the feeling of **ownership or choice** in our outcome. Incorporating opportunities for student voice and choice in their learning successfully does all three, thereby increasing intrinsic motivation to learn.

~

Dave's Thoughts:

I am going to take a slightly different approach to this one. I am not going to cite personal experiences or research. I am going to make this short and sweet. Kids are people. Five-year-olds are people. Seventeen-year-olds are people. I believe that all people should be afforded respect, kindness, and compassion. As such, all people deserve the right to be heard, to be seen, to feel valued, and to be empowered. If you want your voice to be heard, you better believe your students do too. Unlike you, however, students are often limited in the scope and size of their audience. They have limited access to the world. In fact, we are their world. So, let's let them meet their needs the best way we can. Give them a voice. Give them some choice. Let them do things differently than we would. Let them learn from their mistakes. Above all, let them feel like they matter, because they do.

Why do students deserve voice and choice?

 **A Penny for My Thoughts:**

Why do students deserve voice and choice?

A Penny for Their Thoughts:

Chapter 17

Should kids have access to cellphones in school?

Katelynn's Thoughts:

You're in your classroom teaching your heart out, really delivering the lesson, when all of a sudden, a phone starts going off. You stop talking, every kid is looking around, and you find the one student scrambling around trying to make the noise stop as quickly as possible. Their face is bright red, they're crazy embarrassed, and your lesson is now totally off the tracks.

Oh, cell phones. They tend to be a topic that causes teachers to become frustrated and annoyed, coming up with a myriad of ways to keep them out of the classroom. I've seen the cute ideas on Pinterest, just like everyone else. The cell phone jail, the pocket chart to hold everyone's phone individually, and so on.

But instead of banning cell phones entirely, what if we create a culture in our classrooms that encourages our students to bring them and USE them. I know, I know. Some of you are probably shaking your head at the insanity of this idea. But hear me out.

- *When you don't know the answer to a question while you're sitting with your friends, what do you do?*
- *When you're sitting in a PD conference listening to an amazing speaker, what do you pull out to Tweet about it?*
- *When you know you'll need to reference a photo or schedule later, what do you use to take a picture of it?*
- *When something truly incredible is happening, how do you store or share that memory?*

Most of you probably use your phones for all of this. And you don't find anything to be wrong with yourself doing it. So why is it wrong for our students to do this in our classes?

A few years ago, I began telling my students that I wanted them to bring and use their phones in my class. But I made it clear, I wanted them to use their phones for good and not for evil.

We have to remember: when we want our students to exhibit a certain behavior or learn a specific skill, we teach it to them. So that's exactly what I did. I went through the ways they could use their phones and what they could use them for. Instead of running over to the Chromebook cart every time they needed to look up a word, I had them download the Dictionary.com app. When a student forgot their assignment notebook, they took a picture of the homework board. A literature circle group member was absent, so students sent a quick video letting that person know what they worked on during class. Rather than taking 5 minutes to perfectly copy a table of information into their notes, they snapped a photo of the anchor chart to help with an assignment that night.

It changed the culture of my room, and it was entirely for the better. George Couros shares this notion in his book *The Innovator's Mindset.* He consistently says that technology has the capability to transform what we're doing. And honestly, by banning phones from the classroom, I don't think we're really taking advantage of all that they have to offer.

I'd like us to think about the professional development conferences we've attended. Those of us who are connected are usually snapping photos, writing Tweets, or taking Sketchnotes to share out. Even though we're doing this on our phones, we're still engaged in the presentation.

How cool would it be if that was your classroom? You're teaching something in a way that is so incredible, so moving, that your students want to capture it and even share it with more people! That would be fantastic, in my opinion. And something similar happened in my classroom a few years ago.

I had a student in my 8th hour who was high-energy, a little impulsive, and very funny. We had a great relationship—he was my sound effect machine; I'd point to him when something I said needed some extra oomph! and he would deliver. He was absent for a few days in the spring, home sick with the flu that rampaged through 6th grade. My 8th hour rolled around and a girl in my class cannot get her phone to stop going off. I finally walk over and tell her to check it, just to make sure everything is okay. She showed me the screen, and it's our buddy at home trying to Facetime into class. He eventually sent her a text that read:

"I know you're in 8th period. Tell Mrs. G I say hi."

Now, I don't want to make myself out to be this incredible teacher whose students are lining up to come to class. I'm not always on my A game, none of us are. But I can't deny it—this little interaction made me feel good. Here's a student who is at home sick and wants to be in my classroom so bad that he's Facetiming his friend during class. Kind of a cool moment.

My point is this: Our students have a fantastic learning tool at their fingertips. They have a way to store memories and share them out with others. They have a way to create products that demonstrate their learning and understanding in new, exciting ways. We make use of this same tool in ways that improve our lives, personally and professionally. If you had a job somewhere that banned the use of cell phones, and I'm sure many people have, it's likely that you were or would be irritated by that policy. So instead of stripping our students of this ability, we should be encouraging them to capitalize on it in a *positive* way. We consistently talk about being 1:1 and how much more we'd be able to do; if we allow our students to use a device that many already have, it helps us get even closer to that desired ratio.

That said, I know it's not all rainbows and sunshine. There will always be a student who abuses the policy. But that will happen even in the class-room where cell phones are banned. Prohibiting something does not mean it doesn't happen; it doesn't even mean it will happen less. It simply means that students will be more creative in finding ways to get around it, because they are still going to do it. It's unrealistic that every single student will follow every single rule every single day. But when we create a classroom culture that encourages and teaches our students to use cell phones as a tool for learning, we are helping our kids prepare for their lives in a more realistic way.

If you do decide to allow and encourage cell phone use in your classroom, I recommend several things:

- Set specific ground rules. In my class, this meant no video recording me while I'm teaching, no pictures of classmates or their work, avoid tempting apps like Snapchat or text messaging, & during instruction phone should be face-down on top of your desk.
- Carve out some time to talk about digital citizenship. Talk with your students about cyber-bullying and being kind online. Make them aware that anything they put out on the Internet or in a message can be saved forever. Teach them how to be responsible while using a cell phone.
- Find apps that are useful for your content area, become familiar with them yourself, and encourage students to use them! I post a list of apps in my classroom and how they can be used to help with assignments.
- Start a classroom social media account. Parents are on social media, too. They'll appreciate the ability to check in on what's happening in the classroom and they will love it.
- Have a plan for the student who abuses the privilege. There's always going to be that kid (or kids) who are texting Mom and taking Snapchats when they should be working. Be prepared to handle this. In my classroom, their phone has to sit on my desk if they've "used it for evil" three times. They can still use it, but they have to use it at my desk instead of theirs. It's a social contract, and they've abused the privilege. We'll talk about it one-on-one, and make a plan for the future.

Cell phones are a part of our lives. They have transformed our society completely and provided us with a limitless ability to find answers and share content. They are a powerful tool. Many of our middle and high school students have this tool readily available to them, and rather than capitalizing on it, we are banning it from our classrooms. Instead, let's shift our culture and encourage students to use what they have at their disposal, and teach them how to use it to enhance the learning experience.

∼

Dave's Thoughts:

"If kids have a cell phone in my class, they won't pay attention to me."

"If kids have a cell phone in my class, they will use it to cheat."

"If kids have a cell phone in my class, they might record me."

Yes, yes, yes. I can't deny any of these things. But...the truth is, if my class is boring, they will still be day dreaming. If my assessments are generic, rinse and repeat assessments, then they are probably already cheating, and guess what, kids are already repeating your words and mocking you to their friends and family. It's what they do.

But I get it. Kids can be easily distracted by the phone sitting next to them on their desk. The draw of the notification icon was a psychological invention of Facebook, then later mastered by Google, to get users active on their platforms. Shoot, as I am writing this I have my cell phone next to me on my desk and I find myself drawn towards checking it every few minutes. If only I had learned self control earlier on in my life, maybe this wouldn't be such an issue. If only I had learned personal finance in school maybe I wouldn't be in so much debt. If only I had learned...

And that is the point. It is our job to teach desired behaviors. The reality is Pandora's Box has been opened. Kids have phones. Right now, kids have the worst technology they will ever have in their lives. Technology is just going to continue to evolve. We can't act like we are going back. We aren't. It is our job to use the world as we know it, to prepare them for the world they will know.

In our classrooms, let's teach kids how to search for information and then how to analyze that content to create new knowledge. Let's teach kids how to leverage social media to create greater social equity, to enhance their political causes, and to inspire. Let's teach kids how to collaborate, how to investigate, and how to grow. Let's teach kids how to set their phones face down, how to focus for a few minutes at a time, how to resist temptation, and how to stay present in the moment. If we value it, let's teach it.

Let's make sure these kids don't have to tell their kids, "If only someone would have taught me." Teach it, because we know it matters.

~

A Penny for My Thoughts:

Should kids have access to cellphones in school?

A Penny for Their Thoughts:

Part Five

Teacher Voice

[vois] the right to present and receive consideration of one's desires or opinions

— Dictionary.com

In education, teacher voice refers to the values, opinions, beliefs, perspectives, expertise, and cultural backgrounds of the teachers working in a school, which extends to teacher unions, professional organizations, and other entities that advocate for teachers.

— https://www.edglossary.org/teacher-voice/

I therefore suggest that we should focus on the greatest source of variance that can make the difference—the teacher. We need to ensure that this greatest influence is optimised to have powerful and sensationally positive effects on the learner. Teachers can and usually do have positive effects, but they must have exceptional effects. We need to direct attention at higher quality teaching, and higher expectations that students can meet appropriate challenges —and these occur once the classroom door is closed and not by reorganising which or how many students are behind those doors, by promoting different topics for these teachers to teach, or by bringing in more sticks to ensure they are following policy.

— John Hattie, *Teachers Make a Difference*

My past is riddled with embarrassing moments of regret. Things I wish I had said. Things I wish I had not said. Actions better left undone. Thoughts best cast from my mind. I have made a lot of mistakes. I have not always been the leader I attempt to help others become. I have not always been the teacher I wish my kids had. But, it's looking back on those moments that help me move forward. Hopefully, this memory can help you make better decisions than I ever did.

I have earned the state Principal of the Year award. I have earned the state College Educator of the Year award. I have earned my building Teacher of the Year award. I have earned my doctorate degree and have gone to law school. I have had a lot of confidence and a lot of swagger. I have seen myself as better than, as smarter than, as more important than. Than anyone.

As a building administrator, there is often a requirement of sharing school progress as school board meetings. In an attempt to share updates and celebrate success, schools are given the opportunity to highlight their goals, their challenges, their opportunities, and their triumphs. Some schools bring students to showcase. Some schools bring teachers to speak. I brought graphs.

In my second year as a building principal, I was invited to discuss the rapid improvement in student achievement data. In just over 18 months, my school had leapfrogged over close to 800 schools in the state's annual Top to Bottom rankings and the school board was excited to learn how it happened.

I should have invited the hard working teachers who focused their efforts on teaching essential skills. I should have asked the incredible paraprofessionals to share their strategies for targeted intervention and support. I should have celebrated the work of my assistant principal who worked to improve the student culture and climate creating a place where students wanted to work hard. I should have done just about anything other than what I did.

I stood before the school board, the superintendent, and the entire central office staff, clicking through PowerPoint slides, each showing a different graph illustrating all of the hard work I had done. I described the new master schedule I had created. I discussed the new teachers I had hired. I talked about the new curriculum framework I had adopted. I described the new approach to grading I had just implemented. As my presentation drew to a close and I wrapped up everything I had scripted to share, I was asked what should have been a softball question by one of the board members. She asked, "How are your teachers responding to all of these changes?"

I should have discussed how I believe it's more important to get people to weigh in than work to get buy in. I should have shared how we had revolutionized our team meetings to improve our dialogue and discussions around student needs. Instead I said, "Well, my teachers are just my pawns in all of this. They will get moved all over the place and sometimes be put in uncomfortable positions, but everyone knows pawns don't win the game."

Yes, this is an exact quote and yes, I am mortified that I said it aloud. I wish I could say I realized the error of my ways as soon as I said it, but that's not the truth. I honestly believed what I had said. I believed the school was seeing success because of me. I believed that it was my magic that had recruited so many amazing teachers and convinced everyone else to buy into my ways of doing things. I thought that board meetings, and honestly every day at school, was an opportunity for me to highlight how amazing I was. I didn't care what anyone else thought. I didn't care how my plans impacted others. If people didn't agree with me, there were plenty of other places they could go work. These were my thoughts and these were my words.

I am grateful that I had a few critical friends who knew how to also speak honestly and transparently into my life. They heard what I said. They knew what was in my head. They called me out and called me to task. I am grateful that I listened to their voices. My life and my career were changed because of them and my willingness to finally start listening. They were not my pawns. They were my saving grace. I often wonder what kind of impact I could have had if I had started listening sooner. I wonder but will never know. I can only hope that the voices of other teachers are being listened to today and that my mistakes can serve as a gateway to others' success.

Chapter 18

Can I just close my door and do what's best for kids?

Katelynn's Thoughts:

T

he idea of closing the door is something I occasionally hear. It's typically a response to a new initiative that we don't agree with, a rebuttal to a questionable policy, or a way to fight an unwanted change to our practice. I believe that the motivation behind it is that we are the professionals, the ones in the trenches, who know what our kids need. "I'm just going to close my door and do what's good for kids" is something I've said myself, and from what I've gathered, the sentiment is not all that uncommon.

Amidst all the district initiatives, required testing, and things we *have* to do, educators know when practices are becoming detrimental to our students. We instinctively know when things start to harm instead of help, and we do what we can to combat that which is within our control. From my understanding, that's where this phrase comes from. I see it as misguided.

I do not think we should continue practices that are harmful to students because we were told to. Not at all. I take issue with it because I strongly believe we need to do what's best for kids, and then loudly proclaim that to everyone who will listen.

I understand that this will make us unpopular. I understand that it will ruffle feathers. I also understand that it can put our livelihoods in a precarious position. And if that is so, I understand the lack of willingness to do it and the hesitation to be loud about it. This uncertainty and hesitation is not unfamiliar to me, and I'd be lying if I said I hadn't felt it myself.

While I can recognize the difficulty of the situation, I ask you to consider the position we are putting education in by not challenging the system. By presenting complacency when being asked to engage in harmful practice.

When it comes to challenging education, this is my proverbial hill. When a practice is harmful to students, detrimental to their learning, or unjust in any way, I will die on that hill every single time.

We do not make change by closing our classroom doors to do what's best for our kids in secrecy. We cannot combat harmful practices with our silence. Our influence is only as great as our voice, and when we fail to use it, we fail to make progress towards a better system.

Here I will borrow a quote from Cornelius Minor, a fellow educator and leader of educational equity... *"Progress starts at the explosion."*

The notion that we can make change quietly is false. The idea that we can improve the overall health of our educational system behind the closed door of our classroom is not so.

We must absolutely do what's best for our students, but we cannot hide it. We must share the injustices, the harm, that is perpetuated in our school systems. It is vital that we openly, loudly, and actively demonstrate that we are doing what's best for kids. Especially when we are expected to do something different, something that perpetuates inequity or invokes harm to our students.

Educators are professionals. We spend years cultivating our knowledge and skills. We have experience, sometimes decades of it, working with children and learning how to challenge them and teach them and help them grow.

And we must use this professional status, which we have earned and which gives us unique knowledge, to build a better educational system. That absolutely starts in our classrooms or in our roles as educators. But to truly make a change that steers our system away from harmful practices, we cannot stop there. We must proudly share what we know, what we have experienced, what we have seen in our classrooms. It is crucial that we challenge harm when we see it, in the best way that we can. We must use our voices.

We cannot hide behind our doors.

~

Dave's Thoughts:

As I write this, my oldest child is a sophomore in high school. From the moment he gets home each afternoon, he wants nothing more than to just be left alone in his room. He has no desire to socialize with his siblings or to engage with his parents. He thinks he has ALL. THE. ANSWERS. He doesn't feel like he needs to listen to anyone or learn from anyone. He may be a teenage boy, but unfortunately, this description might also sound a lot like some teachers in your school. Doors closed, no socializing, no desire for feedback, no desire to grow.

I get it. When I was in the classroom, I hated having other adults in my room. I did not enjoy having a co-teacher and despised classroom visits from my administration. I was a good teacher. I didn't need help and I didn't need anyone else's judgment. But, wow, what kind of teacher could I have been if I had been more open to discussions, to collaborations, and to growth.

I am a firm believer that almost everything we do in schools is good. As John Hattie discovered, 95% of the things we are doing in our classrooms are good and have a positive impact on kids. Odds are, your classroom is a good classroom. The statistics state that the students in your classroom are probably learning, they are growing, and they are thriving, but are they reaching their potential? Are you? One of the problems with being good is that we often don't become great. When things are OK we don't seek improvement. Just because things are good, doesn't mean they can't be ahemm...good-er. If we expect our kids to seek constant improvement, we need to seek it as well. We know feedback is one of the strongest determinants of success and this goes for you as much as it does your students. Feedback happens when an action is taken and advice soon follows. Take a chance. Try something new. Ask others for their thoughts.

Unless of course you are in an environment where you are expected to stick to a script, to follow a predetermined lesson plan, to teach from a textbook, and are not expected to actually make any instructional decisions or make any impact on kids, ever, then close your door, turn out the lights and teach your heart out. If that's not your circumstance, open your door, invite guests in, and keep growing.

∾

Can I just close my door and do what's best for kids?

A Penny for My Thoughts:

Can I just close my door and do what's best for kids?

 **A Penny for Their Thoughts:**

Chapter 19

Do politics belong in education?

Katelynn's Thoughts:

We spend time in our classrooms every single day with a group of human beings. And we are tasked with such a huge role in shaping their futures—future perspectives, goals, careers. Each day, we are helping our students become the people they will ultimately be. That includes their citizenship and their ultimate involvement in this world. So, inherently, teaching is political. Our students will grow up, a culmination of their collective experiences (including their education), and grow into their beliefs, opinions, and political leanings. We absolutely, 100% need to prepare them for that outcome.

Whenever I make this assertion, a frightening word enters the conversation. **Indoctrination.** It's a powerful word. The concept of teaching a group of people to accept your beliefs without question has an air of force to it. Truthfully, it's a proverbial lightning rod, which makes us want to shy away from it altogether. But we can't.

Indoctrination, by its definition, is to teach others to accept a set of beliefs uncritically, without question. I teach my students not to accept any beliefs, including their own, without question. I teach them that no opinions should be adopted without consideration, without developing a deeper understanding through critical analysis. I teach them that no set of ideals is inherently wrong, but that disagreement and conversation are necessary and make us better. I teach them that our different perspectives are valuable, and that all should be listened to and heard.

Our students come to us and bring a range of backgrounds, some fantastic and some heartbreaking. They are individuals, unique and budding, on the road to realizing their potential and beginning to find their places in the world.

As someone who believes that student voice matters, I encourage my students to share their opinions. I want them to discuss their beliefs with one another, to experience multiple perspectives. I want to broaden their experience of the world, through literature and poetry and research. I want them to gain a deeper understanding of the challenges we face, they face, as they become more active global citizens. I want them to feel comfortable sharing what they think and hearing the input of others around them. I facilitate questions, responses, and respectful conversations surrounding each person's ideas. I also challenge their thinking and encourage them to discover their reasoning or foundation for their ideas. I promote acceptance, respect, and the quest for deeper understanding.

In my mind, that's exactly what educators should be doing. Regardless of the nature of my students' beliefs or opinions, I think they should be explored—by the kids themselves. I think they should also hear the way that others think, and should engage in recognizing multiple different perspectives. I also advocate that they should witness how their beliefs affect those around them, and how their words can influence the people closest to them.

I do not, by any means, indoctrinate my kids. I do not expect them to bend their beliefs or alter their opinions. I do not encourage them to change what they think or adopt an alternate point of view. Ever. That is their decision to make; their own personal evolution through discovery. I do not encourage them to parrot my own beliefs or those of another student. What I do is teach my kids to think critically, analyze information, respectfully engage in conversation, ask questions, and develop their own views.

I encourage disagreement and conversation, because it is vital. True discussion and debate help us expand our thinking and experience, so that we may move forward with more information than we had before. We learn to listen instead of waiting for our turn to speak, to criticize an ideal but not a person, and to separate a set of beliefs from the human being in front of us. We learn to promote equity instead of equality, and to recognize the difference between the two. We see that our words have consequences, and that we have to accept them when we set out to make a point. We learn that concession isn't bad, because sometimes we were wrong and it's not just okay, but even honorable to admit it.

Above all, we learn that questioning and thinking for ourselves are necessary, and that when someone attempts to indoctrinate us with a set of beliefs we do not agree with, we by no means have to give in.

Dave's Thoughts:

As educators we have an amazing opportunity and an enormous responsibility to shape and craft the future. We are entrusted to guide, support, and nurture today's youth to prepare them to be tomorrow's voters and change agents. We live in a society in which we encourage civic participation, empower active voices to be amplified, and desire independent voices to bring about unity. As educators, it is our charge to instill in our students the desire and knowledge of our democratic principles and ideals, while also encouraging independent thought and reasoning. So, do I believe politics belong in education? YES, but do I believe it is our responsibility to teach students what to think? NO. No, in politics, No in science, No, in Math, No, in Language Arts, No everywhere. Our job is to help create students who are jury ready. Students who can sift through facts and evidence, students who can analyze and synthesize. We should be teaching students HOW to think, not WHAT to think.

I hope to instill in the students I teach and lead an ability to critically analyze data, to determine fact from fiction, to use reason to support claims, and have a moral compass that guides action. I hope to play a part in developing future adults capable of serving on a jury of their peers, determining guilt or innocence of their friends, family, and strangers free of prejudice and bias. My hope is that I can help my students learn how to think without indoctrinating them with what to think. I want my students to understand that all people are flawed, all have room for growth, and that all ideas and thoughts come from these same people. I want my students to understand that their teachers are imperfect, so are their parents, and so are they, yet I also want my students to assume the good and doubt the bad. I want my students to have hope for a better future and an understanding that their decisions can help us all get there.

As an administrator I have the responsibility to support my teachers while also protecting my students. Through the years I have had my fair share of parents contact me to complain that their child is being exposed to thinking that is contrary to what is being taught at home. I have had parents claim that teachers are using their platform to corrupt their children. I have had parents claim that teachers are using their influence to sway and persuade students away from family values. These are always claims that I take very seriously, because I firmly believe our role as educators is to support our families and communities. Our job is to stand beside those we serve. However, I am also not a pushover who will always respond to the first complaint I hear, often originating from partial facts and incomplete information.

The reality is, because we live in an amazing country that allows for a democratic process, almost everything is political. From learning about fossil fuels, to classic literature, to the Civil Rights Movement, to Congressional oversight, from our Founding Fathers to the Free Market, the United States is a nation built on politics. It is my responsibility to make sure the students I teach today understand the power of their vote, to take seriously the privilege and responsibility to mark a ballot, and to embrace their opportunity to make this nation as great as they desire it to be. So, do I believe politics belong in our schools? Absolutely. Feel free to exercise your political free will and disagree with me. That's what makes this country great.

A Penny for My Thoughts:

A Penny for Their Thoughts:

Chapter 20

Social media—should we really be sharing?

Katelynn's Thoughts:

Educator use of social media is a popular topic right now, and it tends to be pretty polarizing. Teachers are either completely on board, usually using multiple platforms, or they are staunchly opposed. Whatever side you fall on, I can tell you one thing. Social media can change your life. I say this with total confidence because Twitter completely changed mine.

When I created a teacher social media account, at first I didn't use it that much. I am a younger teacher, but I wasn't a huge fan of social media. A colleague encouraged me to create a Twitter account and join a chat, so I did. I would occasionally login and post a few photos or an overview of what my students were doing. But for the most part, I didn't invest a lot in it.

It wasn't until a few years later that I decided to up my investment. I attended a local conference, and it seemed like everyone there was using hashtags, sharing handles, and creating connections. It was then that I really began to spend some time building my network, participating in Twitter chats, and connecting with other passionate educators.

Over the past few years, my practice has been pushed to new limits because of conversations on social media. I've gotten tons of valuable resources, heard new ideas that I've been able to try, and so much more. It's a wealth of information. It's full of value. It's a great form of professional development. While social media has changed my classroom immensely, the way it's changed my life is even greater.

The beautiful thing about social media is the connection you make with other incredible people. Because of it, I've been able to have one-on-one conversations with powerful practitioners and form friendships that provide me support and help make me better—as a professional and a person. I've been able to connect meaningfully with practitioners who share my passion, but also those who challenge my thinking and force me to confront my own shortcomings and mistakes.

I've also been able to connect with some popular authors, those who have written the favorite books of my students, and help my students connect with them, too. A few years ago, I had a student write a letter to Elly Swartz, telling the author how much her books had changed her life. We couldn't find a mailing address anywhere and we wanted to make sure we could send it physically, so I reached out via Twitter. We got the mailing address pretty quickly, and we were able to create a cool connection with a popular author!

In addition, I've been able to share my own reflections and resources on social media. I'm able to (hopefully) help better the profession as a whole by sharing activities and lessons I teach that cultivate amazing learning for my students. I have an authentic audience that helps me reflect deeply and often through writing. My professional circle has grown immensely, and I can truly say that I am better for it. My classroom is better for it. My teaching is better for it.

Beyond even that, social media is the reason I was able to present at my first national conference in November. If I hadn't participated in a chat, taken a leap of faith, and made a connection, I never would have been there. I literally would not have had that opportunity. And it was an incredible opportunity. I attended an immensely powerful conference where I was able to learn so much. Even though I went alone, I already knew people there. People I had already connected with, talked to, learned from... on social media.

When I say social media changed my life, this is what I mean. I've made friends, developed my practice, and been presented with incredible opportunities.

~

Dave's Thoughts:

Educators in the United States are currently confronted with a major vulnerability for our future. We are facing a teacher shortage, an administrator shortage, and at the same time we are seeing record lows in parent/community satisfaction with our schools. I am a believer that these are all related. As quality teachers leave the profession, fewer quality administrators are available to fill vacancies. As fewer quality administrators are available, schools suffer, satisfaction rates dip, and the cycle continues. So how do we change the cycle? We change the narrative.

When I was a child, everyone got their news from the newspaper. Shoot, my first job was as a paperboy. I was responsible for ensuring my neighborhood was up to date on what was happening and how the local newspaper editors felt about it all. Delivering the paper as a twelve-year old, my lens was limited, but each day I was exposed to the major headlines written "above the fold." Today, most of us only read a newspaper when we stay at a Holiday Inn Express and grab our free copy of the USA Today. Our newspapers have been replaced by Facebook, Twitter, and Instagram. We are the writers of the news and mysterious algorithms are the editors deciding what items appear at the top of our feed and what gets buried "beneath the fold." Public opinion is no longer swayed by professional reporters paid to uncover the truth, but instead by parents, community members, and neighbors who share their versions of reality 240 characters at a time.

It is up to us to change the narrative. Social media is a dated term. To many, it is simply *media*. It is not a place to connect and share socially, but a place to disseminate ideas and spread propaganda. I know there are many organizations who create strict social media policies because of that very reason. They try to prohibit their employees from entering the ugliness that can exist in an attempt to protect them and the reputation of their system. However, this is also similar to the mindset we have seen from nations in the past that censored books, burned those considered contro-versial, and created a focus of reading consistent with one perspective. The power of social media is that it works. The same reason we are often asked to stay away is the same reason I believe we need to actively participate. It works. It persuades. It convinces. It shapes a narrative.

It is up to us to tell our story. Social media is a place for us to celebrate the work we do. To put ourselves on a pedestal. To shine our light and remind the world of the importance of education. Social media is a place to form connections, to build reputations, and to grow as people and organizations.

As I write this, I have 12,200 followers on Twitter, 2,814 friends on Facebook, and 1,253 followers on Instagram. I do not have any blue check marks. I am not considered an Influencer, but I know I have influence. If we believe that the angry mom across town has the power to persuade public opinion against us with one Facebook post, we must also believe that we have the power to create allies, to generate hope, and to change the narrative. We have a shortage of quality educators, today, in part, because of the stories we allowed to be told yesterday. If we want to change the future of our amazing career, it's up to us to help others realize how incredible the work really is. So, pull out your phone, open your favorite social media app, and celebrate the great work one of your colleagues is doing...seriously, now. Before you read any more. Take action. Tell the story. Share the work. Shape the narrative.

Social media—should we really be sharing?

A Penny for My Thoughts:

A Penny for Their Thoughts:

Part Six

Professional Growth

[pruh-fesh-*uh*-nl] making a business or constant practice of something

[grohth] development from a simpler to a more complex stage

— Dictionary.com

"Teaching involves such a complex set of skills that lessons are almost never perfect. The key to being an accomplished teacher is acquiring the skill to continually improve one's practice; an important vehicle for this is reflection and conversation."

— Charlotte Danielson—*Enhancing Professional Practice: A Framework for Teaching*

A Know It All Doesn't Need A Mentor—Katelynn's story

When I walked into my very first teaching job as a bright, shiny, new teacher, I was ready to take on the world. My excitement was palpable and I could not wait to get into my classroom and start working with students. I was also looking forward to building relationships with my colleagues, and was eager to join a team that I had been told was a veritable "powerhouse."

I met my team and started working with the teacher who I was told would act as my mentor. When I started, the district I was in didn't yet have a formal mentoring program, so this partnership was relatively unofficial and the match was made based on proximity and shared grade level content. Our team began meeting regularly, crafting lessons, implementing a new writing curriculum, and discussing our flexible grouping strategies for math class. We problem-solved various issues that came up with our special education team, support staff, and administrators.

I'll never forget how eager I was to show that I had something to offer to those conversations. Feeling like I had to earn my spot and be an active team player led me to speak up in these meetings and share what I could from my limited experience as a student teacher and in my undergraduate classroom.

One day, I went to my mentor teacher's classroom, which was right across the hall, to share my excitement about a lesson that had gone successfully. I was thrilled to share this, as we had just earlier been talking about how we were teaching this particular writing strategy for the first time. I bounded into the room and told him how well the lesson had gone, only to be met with a lackluster nod. Figuring it wasn't a good time, I went back across the hall to prep for the next class.

Later that day, my mentor came into my room to tell me we needed to talk. He brought another of our team members with him, and they both sat down and asked me to join them. The next words he spoke were ones that still reverberate in my head whenever I'm feeling insecure or experiencing imposter syndrome.

"You really come across like a know-it-all."

They went on to tell me that it wasn't my place to share ideas in meetings, but that I should keep my mouth shut and listen to the veteran teachers who knew what they were doing. I was told that I needed to recognize that people did not like how often I shared, and that it would be better if I just let others take the lead. Oh, and when I shared about my successful lesson earlier? Well that had really upset my mentor teacher because *his* lesson had gone well too, and I just completely overlooked that to talk about myself.

I felt like the wind had been ripped from my sails. I was deflated and embarrassed and completely humiliated. When they left, I had three minutes to get myself together before my kids came back from specials, so I quickly got my bearings and went on to finish the day. As I left, I vowed to myself that I would do exactly what they said—keep my mouth closed and listen to the veteran teachers.

Eight years later, this moment still hits me in moments of uncertainty. But what's worse is the impact it had on me for several years after. I shut myself off to partnerships and collaboration, especially with veteran educators, instead preferring to keep to myself. In my mind, if I just put my head down and did the work, it would be better and people would not think so lowly of me. It took quite a while and the influence of a more positive mentor to help me recognize that what I had experienced was not, in fact, mentoring at all. Once I had experienced true mentoring, I could see the damage that experience had in stunting my professional growth. Years later, I've learned that *everyone* has expertise and knowledge to bring to the table—veteran and new educators alike—and that having a mentor to rely on and celebrate with (and event write a book with!) is irreplaceable.

Been There, Done That – Dave's story

I've been around the block. I'm in my third decade as an educator. I have worked in two states, six buildings, and in five districts. Some may look at this and think, "Wow, that's a wealth of experience." Others may realize I just can't ever find a place that fits. I would love to say that as I have aged, I have learned more. I wish I could say my experience has made me better. I regret knowing that since the moment I walked into my first classroom as a new college graduate, I already had all of the answers. Nobody could teach me anything.

Throughout most of my career, I built a moat around myself. I didn't want anyone coming to my self-made castle and offering me any advice or any suggestions. What I was doing was working for me, and it appeared to be working for most of my students. I didn't need any new fads. I didn't need to learn about new tricks. I didn't want to be a part of any pendulum swinging back and forth.

I started my career before instructional coaching was a popular growth model. That's probably a good thing as I would have just pushed everyone away. I believed staff meetings were a waste of my time. I thought guest speakers were glorified sales people. I didn't need new textbooks, new curriculum, or new devices. I had it all, even though I had no one. I had all of the answers, until I realized I had them all wrong.

After almost twenty years as an educator, I worked and taught alone. I didn't need to grow. I just needed others to do things the way I did. This was my true identity, my true beliefs. Thankfully, the last decade has brought healing and revealing. I now have friends. I now have confidants. I now have co-authors. I now am seeing real improvements.

Confident Vulnerability—Our story

Our professional relationship was one that neither of us necessarily expected, and had it happened at different points of our careers, it may not have. Prior to meeting, we both had started actively seeking out people who we could learn from and who could help us grow. Due to our trepidation about people in our own physical spaces, we both went to social media to find what we were looking for.

A big part of social media is the ability to put yourself and your ideas out there, which was an area both of us were fairly comfortable with. Sharing our ideas on social media with a group of strangers allowed us more freedom to be transparent and vulnerable in a way that we wouldn't otherwise do. In the midst of our sharing, we happened across each other's accounts and started listening in a way we hadn't really done before.

We were both able to learn from one another without the pressure of having to respond immediately, impress the other, or even have to engage at all—at least at the beginning. For awhile, this was the basis of our professional relationship. Quietly learning from one another, taking in the wisdom and knowledge the other put out.

Our first real interaction was a very personal one in May of 2020. Dave reached out to ask how things were going since Katelynn had been a little absent on social media for a few months—vulnerable move! This simple act of reaching out to check in opened the door for a bigger conversation —a conversation we agreed to have on Dave's Lasting Learning podcast.

That episode was listened to by thousands of people, many of whom commented on the dynamic and the comfortable banter, which led to the two of us wanting to feed our egos and vulnerable spirits more.

After webinars, conversations, and writing this book together, we've found this professional relationship to be one of the most beneficial and challenging ones we have. While we do tend to be lockstep about certain issues, there are often times when we don't agree or hold the same viewpoint. When this happens, we never agree to disagree. We talk it out with an ever present curiosity about why—Why do you feel like this? Where did your opinion come from? How can I learn from you? Our confident vulnerability in both ourselves and our relationship is what has allowed each of us to grow personally and professionally. Collective efficacy at its finest.

Chapter 21

Does experience matter? Are veteran teachers better teachers? Are newer teachers more innovative?

Katelynn's Thoughts:

S ince I'm a younger teacher, you might be surprised by my response to this. But the answer is yes, experience is incredibly important in education. I do, however, believe that it can take many forms.

A veteran teacher's experiences are wholly beneficial and valuable ones. Many educators who have been in the educational field for years have a wealth of information gathered from their time in the trenches. Most of the things they learn over the years are skills we cannot learn in a teacher preparation class, a Master's program, or really anywhere other than a classroom. This is their strength—their knowledge of the unteachable moments and the lessons they've learned along the way.

On the other hand, new educators have a set of experiences they bring, too. Not only have they (most often) just left a program that was (hopefully) full of the latest content knowledge, technology tools, and curricular advances, but they also bring their own *personal* experiences too. I know that when I graduated from my undergraduate program, I had exclusively used the Common Core standards for math and language arts. That left me with a deep understanding of the standards and how to use them—something veteran teachers were only just transitioning toward using.

The important thing to remember is that every educator—veteran, newbie, novice, all of them—brings experiences to the table. Like our students, we are the sum of our *life experience*. And that background shapes our personality, our identity, and, yes, how we show up in front of students and colleagues every day. Our humanness is our strength; it's what sets us apart from others and allows us to build relationships, craft responsive curriculum, and meet our students where they are. But this only happens when we see it as such.

Instead of buying into the stereotype that all veteran teachers, or boomers (as the kids call it), have an outdated, ineffective approach, we have to tap into their wisdom. The type of wisdom that can't necessarily be taught, but absolutely can be shared. We've got to view those experiences, both in the classroom and outside, as ones that can help us be the best educators we can be. It's also problematic to assume that veteran teachers aren't open to innovation and change. I've known veteran teachers who consume professional literature and research frequently, and who are consistently evolving to meet the needs of the moment.

In the same way, we also have to stop the view of new educators as lost newbies who bring nothing to the table. While they may not have the vast educational background or decades of experience in a classroom, they do have something to offer. Instead of shutting that down, we must encourage them to share their thinking, ideas, and resources. This not only promotes their growth as an educator, but it also provides the group with a range of experiences and different perspectives, which in turn, helps us ensure our practice is the best it can be. New educators might not come in with wisdom, but they do come with experiences, and those should absolutely be valued.

My beliefs on this are deeply personal. Like many, I will never forget my first years in the profession, but for very different reasons. During my second year teaching, I almost left the profession altogether. I had a job offer in a financial advisor's office, and was strongly considering taking it. The reason? I was consistently told that my ideas did not matter and that I should not share them in meetings. That, because I was new, I should just listen to what everyone else had to say. They knew more than I because they'd been teaching longer, so I should keep my mouth shut.

It was devastating. I can only imagine how many other new educators have felt this way, and I'm always curious whether the staggering number of educators who leave the profession in the first few years do so because of a similar experience.

The point is this. Experience absolutely matters. But *all* kinds of experience matter, and *all* educators bring a unique perspective to the table. All voices should be heard and valued. Regardless of status, we have to make use of our best resources—each other. The smartest person in the room is the room.

Does experience matter? Are veteran teachers better teachers? Are newer teachers more innovative?

Dave's Thoughts:

Well, I am fifteen years older than Katelynn, so of course experience matters. I am definitely way smarter than she is. Ha! You already know this isn't true. I mean, as you have been reading, there is a strong possibility that you are resonating with her words a lot more frequently than you are with mine. But, experience does matter.

Our experiences determine who we are, what we think, what we believe, and what we do. Our experiences determine our habits, our behaviors, and often determine what makes us so stubborn.

As a new teacher, two decades ago, I was ready to set the world on fire. I came to work everyday relishing in what some would describe as hero worship as hundreds of 12-year-olds hung on my every word in my middle school classroom. It's crazy how big my ego was able to swell simply because I was able to entertain some pre-teens who felt like I was the smartest person on earth. Because of that, I often felt invincible and felt like that same competence that I brought to the classroom for my students should be accepted just as openly by the adults I encountered daily...boy was I wrong. My own arrogance and belief in myself often caused me to live and work on an island, fighting for the principles that I held true...every single principle.

I was that guy that caused every staff meeting to run thirty minutes overtime because I would challenge the new dress code policy, I would debate the grading scale, I would question the need for yet another fire drill. Nothing was ever good enough, nothing that is, unless it was the way I would do things.

Within a few years that arrogance really began to swell. In my first two years of teaching, I played on my lack of experience to develop practices that I thought were founded on logic and wisdom. By year three, those same practices, and many new procedures and policies, were no longer based on logic, but instead on what was best for me. What I began with the best of intentions, to help students, quickly morphed into what was best for me. My reputation as a teacher slowly shifted from one where I was innovative and fun to one where I was seen as strict and unbending. I no longer debated ideas, but simply believed that my way was the way. After all, my way worked my first two years, it would continue to work every year after. If it didn't, the fault couldn't be mine. The blame had to go to the kids, their parents, the community, the ineffective teachers who taught around me, and any other scapegoat I could manufacture.

This was more than two decades ago, but I think for many of us, this is still our reality today. We became educators because we had a preconceived notion of what school should be, either a replica of our own experience or something new and better than what we endured. We created classrooms based on our visions, procedures focused on our conveniences, and habitual patterns developed out of our past practices. Our experiences determine our beliefs, but they do not need to determine our futures.

Stereotypes exist that novice teachers are more adaptable and flexible and veteran teachers are more stubborn. Likewise, it is often said that novice teachers are less capable while veterans possess more tools. Although there may be semblances of truth to these statements, they are not definitive. Veterans can grow with a willingness to reflect and novices can excel with confidence and determination.

I am all about improvement. At the end of every year, I spend some time reflecting on what my strengths and struggles are so that I can make a plan for progress. At work I spend time evaluating programs, processes, and people. One thing I have noticed recently in schools is that far too many of us say teachers matter more, that the people make the difference, yet we spend so much of our time focusing our improvement efforts on programs and processes. We think of ways to circumvent those who matter more instead of diving deep to develop the real difference makers. We know teachers are the drivers of learning, but we pour money and time into software, classrooms, textbooks, and schedules instead of into the people who make it all happen.

As a sports fan, I often use athletics to try and illustrate my points, so I may as well do so again. LeBron James is considered by many people as one of the greatest basketball players of this era. He is dominant, he can shoot, dribble, pass, rebound, and play defense (when he chooses to). Pretend for a moment that you are a general manager of a team LeBron plays on and you have the task of making the team better. Your goal is to get wins and championships. You can do this by upgrading the concession stands at the arena. You can do this by bringing in new players to circumvent LeBron, players who will not pass him the ball or expect him to be great, or you can do this by bringing in players that complement his game and allow him to dominate. Each of these strategies have been tried on his teams. Some owners and GMs have attempted to distract the fans from what is happening on the court by upgrading the arena and concessions. (I do love a good hot dog and beer, though, so let's not completely dismiss this strategy.) Some have attempted to save LeBron by bringing in others to take the pressure off, and some have brought in players to compliment him and make him even better. Only the latter has resulted in championships, however.

Often in schools we get ourselves distracted by things that don't matter at the expense of those that do. As a leader who has had the opportunity to help lead turnaround efforts in a few schools and districts, I have learned that no program, no paint job, no software will ever impact a child like an amazing teacher. If you are a leader, all of your focus should be on making teachers better, not working around them.

If you have struggling students in your school (we all do), do not go on the hunt of the newest tech gadget to give to the kids. Look for ways to help a teacher work with those students more. If you have accelerated students in your school (we all do), do not look for activities and classes to fill a schedule. Look for ways to have teachers inspire and motivate innovation. Stop looking for ways to work around teachers and begin looking for ways to support teachers.

Support does not simply mean increasing pay. Support means, if you have the option between a new textbook or staff professional development, invest in the teachers. If you have a choice between painting a hallway or developing a teacher, choose the teacher. Always, choose the teacher!

The research is clear. If you want to increase student learning, you have to focus on the teachers. Teachers are the difference makers. Teachers matter more. Teachers provide feedback, establish the culture, set the expectations, develop the assessments, and plan for progress. If you are a leader, spend your time building capacity in teachers, and you will be amazed at the learning that results from your students.

Does experience matter? Are veteran teachers better teachers? Are newer teachers more innovative?

 **A Penny for My Thoughts:**

Does experience matter? Are veteran teachers better teachers? Are newer teachers more innovative?

 **A Penny for Their Thoughts:**

Chapter 22

Does Professional Development matter?

Katelynn's Thoughts:

Professional development is an interesting concept. When some of us hear it, undoubtedly our minds go straight to an all-day conference with a keynote speaker, breakout sessions, and a (hopefully) free lunch. Hastily grabbing the official paper on the way out the door so you can log these hours into your licensure system, and ensuring you meet the requirement come license renewal time. I've attended quite a few of these conferences, and fortunately, a good majority of them have proven to be useful experiences.

I know, however, that they aren't always good. In my time as a teacher, I've also found that these learning days, while valuable, don't always have the sustained effect that I would like. I'll often walk out feeling energized, full of ideas, and renewed in my excitement for this beautiful profession. A few days later, we go back to school and I implement some new strategies, employ some new instructional methods, and add a few new titles to my library. Often, I make a few changes to my practice that are for the better.

But is one or two learning days really enough for educators to feel fulfilled? Is it really enough to sustain us, encourage us to employ new ideas in our practice, and support us as we do so? I'm going to go with no.

In order for professional development to take hold, educators need sustained contact hours, sometimes up to 20 (Garet, Porter, Desimone, Birman, & Yoon, 2001). Seems outlandish and impossible to devote that many hours to sitting in someone's comfortably decorated classroom, reading the posters and bulletin boards that are getting more attention than they have all year. That's because it is. Devoting that number of hours is unreasonable, and for most of our schedules, not even feasible.

So It's time for educators and educational leaders to reconsider what professional development is and what it looks like. I don't just mean restructuring our workshops and faculty meetings. I mean completely overhauling our conception of it. Because the way I see it, we are honing our skills as professional, licensed educators all the time, in a huge variety of ways. But before I start on what professional development is, I want to make a quick note of what it isn't.

It's definitely not:

- Jumping into every new initiative head first
- Negativity toward every new initiative because it isn't what we've always done

Unwillingness to adapt has no place in the educator's arsenal. It can often seem overwhelming when The Next Big Thing gets introduced and I get that, but approaching it with a closed mind is not the answer. Instead of shooting it down outright or justifying the ways you're already doing it so you don't need to change, ask questions and seek out more information.

Because professional development is seeking out your own research. One of my favorite parts of grad school was the access to our online databases. Many of my courses didn't have textbooks (my wallet thanks you), and instead encouraged us to seek out peer-reviewed journal articles instead. I was unsure at first, but as I became more comfortable navigating the robust resources available to me, I was thrilled. There was so much information available to me, information that could truly influence my teaching and my kids, and all I had to do was go out and find it.

It became commonplace for me to refer immediately to our library website when I was seeking out something new. Creating a new unit or a new resource, I'd consult a few research articles on best practice. Looking for behavior interventions for a few of my students, I'd run a quick search to find some ideas. Reading through these journal articles and case studies gave me real, research-based methods to incorporate into my day-to-day teaching. It was readily available when I needed it, tailored to exactly what I was trying to do. Sounds like a pretty personalized PD session that will actually transform teaching and benefit kids. And I didn't even have to travel. When that isn't enough, I refer to my bookshelf.

Reading professional literature is a form of professional development. When a journal article isn't quite enough, or better yet, when you've found an author you really like, professional literature is the natural extension. I've been lucky to connect with a few professional authors, and I'm thankful I did. Between that experience and the influence of some of my colleagues, I've discovered how transformative some of this literature is. There are so many resources and suggestions shared in these books that can be used right away to benefit our students' learning, that it seems like an obvious form of PD to me.

When we engage in study, we often highlight, annotate, or mark pages with post-it notes with applications to our classrooms, or ways that the new ideas will fit in our practice. We refer back to it later, seeking out those hastily written notes, as we plan and adapt our lessons. This clearly demonstrates growing our practice, and improving our pedagogical and/or content knowledge to better our instruction for students. Another hall-mark of professional development.

This desire to read professional lit has been a reflective experience, too. Not only because many of the authors call for it, but because it's left me considering my undergraduate experience and thinking... Man, I should've read the book.

Blogging is a deeper form of reflection, and definitely a way to develop professionally. I could write a book about this. It's something I believe in because I've experienced firsthand the profound effect it's had on me as an educator.

Sitting down to write a piece, whether it be about my classroom or my philosophical beliefs, requires a deeper level of reflection than normal. Writing forces me to fully process a lesson I taught and consider why I did it that way. It brings my philosophy to the forefront and makes me think through the foundation for this belief. It's even caused me to change my mind about stances I was adamantly in favor of. The notion that an audience will be looking at my piece encourages me to think more critically about what I do and what ideals I subscribe to. Without the platform of my blog, a lot of this reflection wouldn't take place at the same level... or at all. Being a reflective educator is a deeply personal experience, but is a necessary part of developing professionally.

Beyond just writing a piece, there's the interaction. There's a community involved when you start a blog, and it tends to have a positive influence on you as a professional. The audience isn't just an unknown body of nothingness. When I write, I write to and for real people, and many of you engage in conversations with me based on what I've said. Some of my colleagues at school follow my writing and also chat with me, or challenge me, about what I put out there. And I love it. Because it engages us in professional conversation and collaboration. Which is yet another crucial aspect of PD—the learning community. Group interaction often lends support and stimulus to our development, especially when we try something new. We often need a second set of eyes, guidance from someone who's tried it, or even just the knowledge that we're not in it alone. When something goes well, it's a huge source of encouragement to put it out there. When something completely flops, it's comforting to know that there are still educators out there offering support. It's vital to have this collaboration, and fortunately, blogging can be one source of it.

Another source is probably my favorite form of PD... Twitter. I. Love. Twitter. I tell educators constantly that if they aren't on Twitter, they are missing out on the greatest collective source of PD that exists. Because, honestly, that's what #edutwitter is.

Engaging in Twitter chats is powerful stuff. Connecting with educators around the globe and discussing ideas, books, practice, culture, disruption of social norms, available resources and MORE is an incredible way to become a better educator. It builds a community united around a common purpose and sense of responsibility, and is by far the best way to build a professional network.

I have learned more than I could ever say from educators on Twitter. I've established and been able to maintain professional relationships with teachers all over the world. I have been offered new opportunities to engage in study and research through connections I've made on this platform. It's real. And it's full of generous, wickedly smart individuals who are dying to share their practice with you. Literally all the time. And you can do it in your pajamas. Definitely a win.

It's clear that there are an insane number of professional development opportunities out there. So many that I couldn't possibly cover all of them. Educators as a whole are a passionate bunch, devoted to the learning of our students. We are constantly bettering ourselves, looking for ways to do this important work to the best of our abilities. I firmly believe that the overwhelming majority of us seek out opportunities like these consistently, simply because we want to provide the absolute best education possible for our students. Every single time we do this, we are growing as professionals. Every single time, we are engaging in professional development.

Even if the hours don't count toward our license renewal.

~

Dave's Thoughts:

There are so many things I want to say about this, but I am biting my tongue, or more accurately, sitting on my hands. It's ironic in a book like this, I know, but stick with me for a second.

I have been an educator for more than two decades. I have been a classroom teacher, a building administrator, a central office administrator, and a college professor. I have had my fair share of opportunities to participate and lead professional learning opportunities. I have seen a few things that work and have seen many things that fail miserably, most of which I was responsible for. PD (Professional Development) is at the heart of what we do as life-long learners. We are constantly seeking opportunities to develop and grow. We are on a quest to improve and evolve. Even your willingness to read this book and participate in the conversations around it demonstrate that, and that is why I believe PD matters. However, I also firmly believe the model we use to deliver quality professional learning and development opportunities is broken and needs an overhaul in many places.

What we do, they do. This is a mantra I live by as a leader. Have you ever heard of mirror neurons? It is because of mirror neurons in our brains that when a person near us yawns, we yawn. Mirror neurons explain why a baby in a crib smiles when she sees her mom or dad smile. They explain why people in the south all say, "y'all" and those in New England say "you's guys." Mirror neurons are our brain's way of conforming to those around us and helping us assimilate to our surroundings. Similarly, they are why when we have PD experiences that involve a sit and get model with an expert telling us what we need to know, we get sit and get lectures in our classrooms. They are why we get classrooms with teacher created policies and procedures instead of norms created by our learners, when we have schools and districts with admin created handbooks instead of collaborative plans.

Does Professional Development matter? Yes, I think PD matters, for the same reason I think parenting matters in schools. Kids become like those they are surrounded by the most and so do we. If we want engaging, inspiring, relevant, and enduring educational experiences, then we need to create those for all of our learners, not just the kids. Who we are is who they will become. What we do, they will do. We need to keep learning, not just so we can gain more knowledge and more exposure to content, but so that we can be exposed to innovation, engagement, empowerment, and risk taking. We need to see in our peers what we hope to see in our students. Does it have to look the same way for everyone? Does it need to be delivered from a stage, in a staff meeting, or in an auditorium? Should it come from the experts among us or from those who have a full-time job of studying the research and practices on display outside our four walls? Only you can decide that, but recognizing that none of us has all of the answers and all of us have the ability to keep growing if we simply allow others an opportunity to pour into us, is key.

A Penny for My Thoughts:

A Penny for Their Thoughts:

Chapter 23

Do we all have to grow the same way?

Katelynn's Thoughts:

Comparison is a tricky one, and with the age we live in now, it is easier than ever to compare ourselves to every educator out there. The rise of social media has resulted in an incredible amount of positives, and I am the first person to contend that we should share resources and ideas with our colleagues at any opportunity. It is worth noting, however, that this sharing does not always mean a new age has dawned, and we all need to jump on board in the very same way, lest we be left behind.

Educators, much like our students, bring a uniqueness into our instruction. The very best of us are inimitable, and that translates into the way we instruct, interact, and engage with our kiddos. Because of this, not every new initiative is going to speak to us, nor will it look exactly the same in every single classroom. The process we take may vary in the amount of time it takes, the journey we take to get there, the background knowledge we need to develop... just like our students' learning.

We have a fatal flaw, as educators. Our willingness to experiment with new things is what makes us so versatile, so incredible at our jobs. But the feeling that we absolutely have to attempt every new experiment at the *same* pace, knowledge level, and level of enthusiasm as our colleagues can be our downfall. The way we have to compare ourselves and our progress to others is not helping us or our students. It's incredibly valuable for us to take a step back and approach anything with a lens of personal growth, taking the time we need to really investigate.

The fact of the matter is that we won't all be in the same place at the same time, and that's beautiful. It's what makes our collaboration so effective and so beneficial. It's why we end up with educators who bring their *different* expertise to the table, lifting our entire profession up as we go. And it's how we forge new paths, ones that will continue to pave the way for those who come after us.

Because our growth is different, and when we accept that, we find so many fantastic ways to go about it.

～

Dave's Thoughts:

In schools, are we charged with creating students who are specialists or generalists? Should we be asking students to decide their future career while in sixth grade, while developing an Educational Development Plan (EDP), so that they can select the right electives, get put on the right track, enter into the right magnet school, go to the right college, get the right degree, and ultimately get the one career we have set them up for so they can do the same job for the rest of their lives, or should we be equipping them to learn, grow, evolve, change their minds, and be well-rounded enough to do anything they want to do?

As I write this, I am in my mid-forties and can emphatically say there is no way I would allow a twelve-year-old to determine my career plans and future. I would not seek the counsel of a sixth grader and ask him, "What should I do with my life?" But looking back on my middle school years, that's exactly what my educational system attempted to do. It attempted to take me as a twelve-year-old and put me on a designated path so that my entire life was scripted in front of me. The truth of the matter is, the world needs people who are not only specialists, but people who are able to transfer knowledge, find cross discipline connections, and learn and unlearn all the time. When we create specialists, we create people who believe they are supposed to be experts in one thing and struggle to receive feedback and ask for support in others.

The educational system in every state in the United States is built on the faulty premise that content area specialists make better teachers than generalists. Educators, the vast majority of whom identify their chosen career while in college, or before, are asked to declare a major, a preferred grade level, and then pass a test to earn a select certification, carving out their role identity, all by the age of twenty-two. At the age of twenty-two, the prefrontal cortex (the part of the brain responsible for reasoning and logic) has not fully formed. Individuals at that age are not able to even secure a rental car due to higher incidents of reckless driving, yet it's at that age that we are setting up the next generation of life changers to carve out their specified and unique career path that we expect to sustain them for thirty-plus years. We then get shocked when we read stories like one recently published in *EdWeek* stating that 54% of teachers claim they are likely to leave the profession in the next two years. Teachers change their minds, realize they need other opportunities to feed their passions, and instead of supporting their growth and evolution, we tend to look at growing these amazing individuals by feeding them a larger and larger stack of content knowledge based on what they were interested in when they were barely old enough to buy a bottle of wine.

If we want to encourage teachers to better themselves professionally, we have to recognize their growth personally. If we believe that students become like those they see most often, we will only create a generation of future leaders well versed in many disciplines if we allow teachers to model this behavior and mindset.

To be bold, I believe that a great teacher can teach anything. They recognize the pedagogical tools that inspire, engage, and inform. I don't, however, believe that any content expert can be a teacher. Disagree with me? Think about your college professors. As a current professor, I can state emphatically that teaching is not the strong suit of most of my peers, although most are brilliant in their disciplines. If we want to develop teachers who are able to inspire a generation to believe, to push boundaries, to innovate, and to create, we must allow teachers to explore, to dream, and follow their passions as well. This doesn't happen when we force every teacher to follow the same learning path, to be exposed to the same development opportunities, following a prescribed scope and sequence. We recognize every student deserves differentiated instruction. We know every child comes to our classrooms with different life experiences and unique knowledge bases, requiring diversified instruction, and so too do teachers within a school. A common certificate does not equate to a common understanding. A common degree does not equate to a common passion.

The bottom line is, if we want teachers who are willing to stay in the profession long enough to become experts, we must allow teachers the opportunity to become generalists. If we want teachers who are able to inspire students to learn specialized content, we need to allow teachers to learn how that content applies to the rest of the world. If we want teachers who are able to change destinies, we must embrace the fact that our teachers' destinies can be changed as well. Teachers, take charge of your own learning and find your own unique path towards developing professionally and personally.

~

Do we all have to grow the same way?

A Penny for My Thoughts:

Do we all have to grow the same way?

A Penny for Their Thoughts:

Part Seven

Change

[cheynj] to make the form, nature, content, future course, etc., of (something) different from what it is or from what it would be if left alone

— Dictionary.com

"Leading in a culture of change does not mean placing changed individuals into unchanged environments."

— Michael Fullan, *Leading in a Culture of Change*

"Change is a continuous process. Therefore it can perhaps best be considered as a series of destinations that lead to further destinations."

— Jody Spiro, *Leading Change Step by Step*

When we really stop to consider it, education as a whole has evolved, grown, and been revolutionized. We've taken huge strides, some of these changes coming about in just the last few years. Some of us are optimistic about the changes, while others of us yearn for the days gone by. Wherever your stance, our resilience and our ability to adapt is incredible. I'm in awe of educators everywhere for how well we've handled the changes we've had to make.

And when I look at these changes—changes we've been thrown into, whether we were ready or not —I'm not only impressed. I'm curious. Some of this might be a natural predisposition to question and wonder, but regardless of where it comes from, I can't help but wonder... if these are the changes we made when we *had* to, what could we accomplish if we *wanted* to?

The possibilities are endless and I'm sure your imagination, like mine, runs wild with the implications of what we could do. As we think about some of the big, controversial, buzzword-worthy topics, I'm reminded of just how far our influences reach. Because the reality is that much of the change that needs to occur has to do with society and institutional problems that have existed for years before us.

But change doesn't start with society. It starts with you and with me and with our *want,* our desire to make that difference. Our preparedness to challenge and evolve. Our willingness to have hard conversations with ourselves and others. Our disposition for growth and readiness for revolution.

Change happens when we make it happen, not while we're waiting for it.

Chapter 24

Why do things always have to change?

Katelynn's Thoughts:

hange is frightening. As someone with anxiety, I crave structure and control. When things continuously change, time and time again, I lose that which I crave. I feel like the ground is constantly moving underneath my feet, and each time I begin to get my footing, it moves again.

But without change, we lose the one aspect of humanity that has resulted in some of our greatest inventions, solutions, and theories. Without change, we have no innovation.

Change puts us in a position where we have to make a choice. We can either choose to embrace the change and adapt, or we can resist, usually to our downfall. When we embrace the change, we open the floodgates of our own creativity and begin to innovate. We open ourselves up to the possibility of something new and better, something that has the potential to transform us.

Education is never constant. It can't be. Change is inherent in the profession, even down to its structure. Each year, a new group of students enters your classroom, and that in and of itself is a change—and it's only the beginning. Among new research being conducted all the time, discoveries of improved best practice models, and even new instructional technology, there is always change on the horizon. And these changes, like all changes, have the ability to revolutionize the profession.

I don't know about you, but being part of an educational revolution sounds pretty awesome to me. While I might be anxious about the how and the what, I know that whatever change may come, my why will remain the same. **I am here to help my students become the people they will ultimately be**. And if any change aligns with that purpose, or better yet, helps me achieve that goal more effectively, that I am jumping in head first.

Dave's Thoughts:

I have been an educator for more than twenty years and have spent more than half of that time as both a building and a district administrator. I have worked in urban schools, rural schools, and suburban schools. I have worked in buildings with PTA members knocking down the doors and have worked in buildings where we struggle to even get a working phone number for our parents and guardians. I have worked with schools that are identified as excelling and in schools that are labeled as failing. In spite of all of these differences, for some reason, politicians and rule makers continue to look for silver bullets and magic pills. They tend to believe there is AN answer that will solve the struggles ALL schools face. They believe that schools, all schools, should simply mimic the behaviors of the schools in the affluent zip codes and success will automatically follow.

Now don't get me wrong. I believe fully that all schools have room to grow and improve. I believe schools should always be looking for ways to excel and evolve. I spend a lot of my time actually traveling the country helping schools identify practices and programs that can yield a great return, but I am also a firm believer that as long as we keep looking for THE answer, we will never find it.

As I typically do, let me explain this with a metaphor.

Back in 2019, I was training to run in the Boston Marathon to raise money for The Leukemia and Lymphoma Society. I am definitely not an elite runner as the vast majority of Boston participants are, but I also didn't want to make a fool of myself. As a result, I attempted to lose 7 lbs over the last six weeks of training, to help me meet my time goals. I knew that losing a few more pounds would help me pick up my pace. On average, I eat about 2500 calories a day. For those last few weeks, I planned on decreasing my caloric intake to about 2000 calories a day knowing that this deficit would help my body begin to burn body fat to compensate.

In the time since that training cycle, I have come to realize that the human body is an amazing thing. Our metabolisms are complex and very smart. After completing the race, I continued with a diet of 2000 calories for a few months and began to see a decrease in my results. As a matter of fact, if I made the decision to continue this caloric intake for the next twenty years, I would not continue to lose weight until I withered away into nothingness. Eventually, my body would adjust to this new normal and my weight loss would plateau. If I want to keep losing weight, I would have to keep shocking my body by adjusting my caloric intake every few weeks to keep my body guessing.

I think schools are a lot like our metabolism. I have seen far too many schools go all-in on a new approach, a new program, a new philosophy and see quick returns. (Think—The Biggest Loser-quick returns...but can they be sustained over time?) These schools then enter year two, three, or four of their pursuit and begin to realize that their momentum has slowed or even regressed. They continue pushing harder, thinking they just need more discipline, more FIDELITY (I am growing to hate that word), more scripts, more pacing, and more compliance. In the meantime, the students, the teachers, the parents, begin to feel like they are going through the motions, they are on the treadmill of work, seeing no real returns on their investment.

I am a believer that if schools want to see continued success, what they need is not a more focused effort on the status quo, but a determination to keep shocking the system. Teachers don't need more scripts and mandates. They need more freedom to experiment, to take risks, and to do something they have never done before. If we want our schools to be healthy, to lose the extra weight they have been carrying around for years, we need to afford them the discipline to be innovative, not just compliant.

∽

Why do things always have to change?

A Penny for My Thoughts:

Why do things always have to change?

A Penny for Their Thoughts:

Chapter 25

There's so much to change, but what if it all fails?

Katelynn's Thoughts:

My experience in education hasn't been decades long, but it has been full of change and growth. The evolution I've gone through has been extensive, including philosophical changes, shifts in my mindset, and entirely new instructional practices. When I reflect on my growth, it's exciting to see where I am now, but at times, startling to think about where I started. It's hard to admit our setbacks and failures, and I can assure you I've had quite a few. But it's in those low moments, those times of defeat, that we usually learn the most. And it's important that we don't let that deter us from continuing to evolve. Because the only way we can truly grow as educators is to be innovative and take risks.

It sounds so simple, but it's not. At all. Taking risks is hard because it requires us to get uncomfortable. It necessitates leaving behind some of our older, familiar practices or philosophies to try something new... something we're unsure of, something different, and something that might not work. The most difficult part is entering into uncharted territory, blazing the trail ahead of us, with no roadmap and no guarantee for success.

Naturally, we shy away from that.

The notion of failure is a powerful deterrent, especially when the cost involves such important factors as our students' learning, parents' reactions, and administrators' irritation. I have been hesitant or unwilling to take certain risks myself because of these potential drawbacks, and have avoided making some changes because of my own fear of failure. It's tough work to get uncomfortable, made even tougher because our stakes are so high. Getting past this barrier requires us to go against our instincts of avoidance, develop our knowledge, and tread carefully into the unknown, often by ourselves. Each time I decide to move forward, to take the risk, it's because I've stopped to consider one compelling question...**But what if it works?**

This question helps me think through my reasoning, my why, for even considering the risk in the first place. It sheds light on the very foundation of my idea, helping me move past the uncertainty and fear of failure. That's not to say the risk yields great reward; sometimes I flop anyway. But it helps me try the new thing, overcome my hesitation, and jump in. And even if it does go wrong, I still have a valuable learning experience and an opportunity for significant growth.

When I first began working toward creating a more personalized learning experience for my students, I was nervous. I loved the idea of providing choice within my units of study, and allowing my students' voices to be heard. I didn't know how to get started, but I had heard of the concept called self-pacing. Student self-pacing models allow kids to choose what they work on each day and how long they need to devote to their tasks of choice. The potential for differentiation within this structure was particularly attractive to me. That year, I had a group of students who were significantly unique in their need for support, and I was struggling to find ways to meet them where they were. So, hearing about this structure, I knew I'd like to try it, but was overcome with this fear of how it could go horribly wrong. What if I let them choose their pace and they had no idea how? What if they chose activities that were too easy or too difficult? What if they finished so quickly that I had nothing else for them to do? What if they were all doing different things at different times? How would I help them all then? What if I completely lost control of the classroom?

I struggled for awhile, arguing with myself that the risk was too great, they wouldn't be able to handle it, and it certainly would not work. I considered adjusting multiple units so they would follow this self-pacing model, and ended up not doing it because I was afraid it would fail and didn't want to ruin the unit. I could not get past the discomfort of the change, especially when it was my second year teaching the same subject in the same classroom with the same team. It was familiar, I had consistency, and that had never happened to me before. I didn't want to give it up.

Finally, we came to our culture literature circle unit. I had learned about self-pacing in November, it was now March, and I'd been mulling it over in my head for every single unit. Every time, going through the laundry list of **what if** questions that ultimately led me to sit back and stay comfortable. This time, as I ran through the questions in my head, the small, unsure question popped up... **but what if it works**?

I thought through how powerful, how useful it would be, for my students to work this way. I reflected on the group I had, how far they had come since the beginning of the school year. I did a little reading on self-pacing, how it increased student motivation. And I decided to go for it. We were going to do self-paced lit circles, and it was going to be great!

Spoiler! It wasn't great. Not even a little. The first week of the lit circle, I gave my students the list of tasks they needed to get done, the mini lessons I would teach if they needed it, and the lowdown on self-pacing. They could choose what they would work on, when they would do it, and take as long as they needed on each task. They had to check in with me at the end of the week to ensure they were working steadily, maintaining a pace that would enable them to finish the unit successfully before spring break.

Disastrous is the only way I can describe that first week. Kids were confused, unprepared, and as my fellow middle school teachers can attest, dreadful at managing their own time without support. My risk, one I had contemplated for months, had not paid off at all. Before I decided to try the self-pacing model, I was consumed with the idea that my entire unit would be ruined if it didn't work out. The kids would learn nothing, parents would be contacting me constantly, administrators would see my out of control classroom, and I would most certainly be fired.

None of that happened, thank goodness. By Tuesday, *one day* after attempting this new structure, I had devised a new method. Based on my students' uncertainty and lack of planning ability, I knew I hadn't prepared them well enough to pace themselves through a week, let alone an entire unit. So, I did what any teacher would do, and found a way to scaffold. I created a weekly calendar with our class times and a checklist of each activity, mini lesson, or task my students needed to complete by the end of the week, which gave them a better balance of structure and choice.

WEEK 1   NAME:

LEARNING GOALS

I can find out the meaning of words & phrases by understanding the figurative and connotative meanings.
I can explain the effect that word choice has on meaning and tone.
I can engage in collaborative discussions based on what I read, building on others' ideas & expressing my own clearly.

TASKS TO COMPLETE

- ❑ Write a definition of the word culture.
- ❑ Read section 1 with pink, blue, & yellow post its.
- ❑ Informal discussion of section 1: first thoughts, etc.
- ❑ Read section 2 using pink, blue, & yellow post its.
- ❑ Determine the setting of the novel as a group.

- ❑ Start adding to personal vocabulary list.
- ❑ Setting research task.
- ❑ Informal discussion of section 2: setting research sharing.

Monday 2/17	Tuesday 2/18	Wednesday 2/19	Thursday 2/20	Friday 2/21
No School!	Tasks to work on in class 1st half:	Tasks to work on in class 1st half:	Tasks to work on in class 1st half:	Tasks to work on in class 1st half:
	2nd half:	2nd half:	2nd half:	2nd half: **Library Friday Reflection**
Homework:	Homework:	Homework:	Homework:	Homework: **Friday Reflection**

I wasn't encumbered by the fact that I had failed, which is one of the tricky aspects of risk-taking we forget about in the insecurity of *Before*. Often, when it fails, we reflect on what happened and find a way to fix it. We do not dwell on the failure, because we cannot. Our students are relying on us to show up, so we do. And so, learning from my failure, I created a new plan. It provided some structure to the model, some scaffolding on organizational skills, while still maintaining the choice and student-centered approaches that boost intrinsic motivation. This calendar pacing strategy I created to remedy this failure is one that I use now, for almost every single unit I teach.

Had I not decided to take the risk, had I not considered what would happen if I was successful, I never would have found one of the most useful strategies I provide my students. I would not have been inspired to try more components of personalized learning, and I would not have found the power that comes with including student voice and choice the way that I did. I may have discovered this later (I like to think that I would have), but I cannot be sure that I would have had the same mindset and philosophical shift.

The beauty of taking risks lies in the evolution that it inspires. It's a hidden beauty, one that we can rarely see before we decide to embark. But when we ask ourselves that one question, we can get a little glimpse of what it might be.

$\sim$

Dave's Thoughts:

If you watch the media, or listen to a lot of our politicians today, you will hear that a lot of people believe that our K-12 public education system is broken, that educators are not doing their jobs, that kids are leaving the systems unprepared for the workforce, and that as a result major overhauls are needed. In my home state of Michigan, over the last two decades, we have lost more than a million students of school age, yet the number of public school buildings has almost doubled. We have a teacher shortage impacting every district in the United States and as a result have more accountability measures in place, driving even the best teachers away. In our quest for differentiated instruction and individualized learning, the average student in America today spends twenty days of the school year being assessed, typically not to plan for instruction, but instead to predict future assessment results. The truth of the matter is that our schools are not broken; they have a disease.

Many of us have never looked at the word "disease" before and broken it down into its root and prefix. This word does not necessarily indicate a virus, a germ, or mutation is present. It literally means a lack of ease. It indicates things have gotten too complex. It describes a state in which there is no balance, no equilibrium, and a lack of systemic focus. Our schools today often suffer from a dis-ease, not because of a lack of quality, but because of a lack of ease. We have made things way more complicated than they need to be. In our attempt to solve the problems, we have created such a sense of misalignment that we have often just made the problem worse.

So what do we need to do to solve the problem? Well, contrary to popular belief, I would argue we need to simplify things and stop getting lost in all the weeds. We have too many programs, too many gimmicks, too many people who proclaim to be experts, too much compliance, and not enough simple teaching, loving kids, and facilitating their passions and innovative mindsets. We are taking too many pills. Before kids are of school age, they are curious, questioning, and playful. As they enter our systems, we make them compliant, rule following, and often silent. As teachers enter the profession, they are inspired, hungry, and ready to change the world. As they continue through their career, we often have the same impact on them, making them compliant, rule following, and silent.

To cure the dis-ease, we do not need more rules, more programs, more assessments, or more accountability. We need to bring back the ease. We need to encourage teachers to embrace the art of teaching. We need to allow teachers to be creative again. We need to develop programs that focus on the interests of students. We need to make sure our kids are happy, supported, and inspired. It's really that simple.

So, no, our schools are not broken, but they are diseased. If we want to fix them, the answer isn't more charter schools, more accountability, and more complex analysis of curriculum requirements. The answer is to bring back the ease. If we want to fix our schools, let's get back to the basics. It's not just reading, writing, and arithmetic; it's about trust, love, passion, compassion, and innovation. That's the cure.

There's so much to change, but what if it all fails?

A Penny for My Thoughts:

There's so much to change, but what if it all fails?

A Penny for Their Thoughts:

Chapter 26

Why does it all matter?

Katelynn's Thoughts:

In education, we have many problems. Educators at all levels: teachers, administrators, district leaders... we are very well aware of the myriad of issues we face. But whenever I consider the biggest problem in education, I can boil it down to one word. Inequity.

I say this because I've studied how education impacts the social mobility of our students. I read a lot of material in a subject outside of my normal field, mainly because my entire perception of education was dismantled a few years ago. I used to believe that education is the great equalizer and that a good education elevates people to a more successful future. But the truth is pretty clear. It doesn't. At least not the way it's currently structured.

Because, as it stands, our educational system has inequity baked right into its fiber. As uncomfortable as that is, it's a truth that cannot be ignored. In order to better understand this truth, I ended up in the field of economics. Specifically, I focused on how this branch of the social sciences discusses education. Because economics, while typically considered the study of money, goes much further. It's really the study of human behavior, wealth, and social mobility, all of which I thought could be remedied with a strong education. But time and time again, many economists have shown evidence that this is a fallacy.

The five economists I've been reading recently are widely known, and four of them are Nobel Laureates. Their credentials are impressive, their research extensive, and they all say the same thing about education. It's not the equalizer many of us believe it to be.

Our educational system is not helping people find better, more successful lives. It is not increasing social mobility and allowing those from underprivileged backgrounds to realize a higher quality of life. In reality, it's exacerbating the problem by perpetuating the inequity that exists in our society. It's continuing to advantage a specific group of people: the rich and white. And the problem in large part is due to its foundation and structure.

Both in the United States and internationally, the curriculum and organization of schools dates back to education's colonial background—the time when schools were designed to train an elite class. According to two Nobel Laureate economists, Banerjee and Duflo, this structure is a remnant from when the purpose of education was to *maximize* the gap between the members of society and the rest of the population (2011).

We see this now repackaged in a different format. The focus is consistently on the future. On providing students the knowledge they need to gain admittance to top universities. Because only this will propel them forward into a successful future with a substantial income. Only this will guarantee their place in society and in the middle or upper class. Doesn't sound too bad, right?

I didn't think so either. We want to provide our students with a quality education that will help them realize their potential and have a comfortable life. The problem, however, goes so much further than that. Thomas Piketty, whose work looks at 250 years of wealth distribution, found that the real predictor of a student's access to a great university isn't their education or ability. It's their parent's income. And it's an almost *perfect* predictor.

A reason for this is because income determines one very important factor: housing. And housing determines the way public education is funded in the United States. Local property taxes are heavily relied upon by the K-12 educational system.

This means that those who live in poor communities consistently get a worse education with fewer resources than those in richer areas, a finding reported by Joseph Stiglitz—in just 2019.

The neighborhood a child grows up in is integral to their future mobility, or ability to move beyond their circumstances. This constraint is linked to the local funding structure. According to Banerjee and Duflo (2011), the places in the most desperate need of high-quality education are the least able to fund it. And the burden of improvement is almost always placed on those in the worst position to make it happen.

Banerjee and Duflo also speak of the influence of income in a different way. While the payoff for education is the same for two students, one will get less education because of his poorer parents. Not just because poorer neighborhoods already have less to spend, but because they have to distribute *less* funding to *more* children. This is because at higher income levels, families tend to have fewer children. Which means that education spending per child grows much faster and is certainly not equally distributed, guaranteeing that wealthy children will get more education regardless of talent, and talented poor children are likely to be denied a chance.

Banerjee and Duflo (2011) also state that, "This is the opposite of what we would expect in a world where education is an investment like any other, unless we are willing to believe that the poor are just incapable of getting educated" (p. 81).

We see this over and over in the education world. Schools with a lack of books, lack of technology, lack of teachers, and overall lack of resources are concentrated in poorer areas. They are overburdened, without counselors or psychologists to help students navigate their mental health. These same schools are located in areas with limited access to libraries, food, and quality health care. And these students are coming to school with their basic needs unmet, meaning they have to go even further and work even harder in worse conditions. All this, just to *have a shot*.

This translates to students from poorer backgrounds being less competitive in an already competition-driven system. And they are at a disadvantage in the race for a successful future before they even enter a school building.

If that's not the definition of an inequitable system, I'm not really sure what is. Paul Krugman even calls this system an oligarchy where wealth is highly concentrated in the hands of a small, privileged group. The common, polite way of addressing this issue is to argue that we need to increase funding to our educational system. Frankly, I disagree.

Education doesn't need *more* funding. It needs a *better funding structure*. One where we don't continuously disadvantage those in the greatest need, while offering ever-increasing advantages to those at the top. But to address this can be uncomfortable. In the words of Paul Krugman, it's far more comforting to state that we must increase funding for education because it assumes that no one can be blamed for the inequitable system. It's to stop avoiding it and address the issue.

Centuries have shown us that this is a problem. And, for centuries, we've pushed it aside. Because it's really, really hard to change an entire system. Especially when it's been in place for so long. And it's even harder when the people you need to get on board to effect the change are the very people the system continuously advantages. But we cannot continue to let this slide. When we do, we become part of the problem. We engage in the perpetuation of inequity.

While we might not be able to make big, structural change tomorrow, we can take some small steps today. We can educate ourselves and engage in study, which will allow us to better understand the fixes that need to occur. We can ensure we are adequately prepared to engage in conversations about the problematic structures that exist within the system, inviting others into this learning. We can challenge practices and beliefs that are fundamentally harming our students and exacerbating the problems we know are there. We can love our students, continue to show up for them every day, and be a positive force for change within the educational world.

But what we cannot do is stay silent. We won't. Because educators already know what these economists show in their data and prove over and over again.

Every kid deserves a chance.

～

Dave's Thoughts:

Every state in the United States has a compulsory education law on its books. Students from age six to age sixteen, by law, have to attend school, receive an education, be assessed on their academic progress, and receive a high quality education. Laws such as these were put on the books, not so much to protect the happiness of individual students or systems, but as a way to protect the durability and elasticity of our economy and our national security. An educated workforce is the foundation for a productive workforce, but the question now is, are our school systems still aligned and prepared to meet this demand?

In direct contrast to the news stories we have heard recently, I would challenge that America does not have a college admissions crisis. As a matter of fact, according to the Organization for Economic Cooperation and Development (OECD), The United States trails Russia, Ireland, Norway, New Zealand, Australia, Denmark, Israel and Belgium—as well as Luxembourg, the United Kingdom, France and Sweden, in college degree attainment.

Furthermore, the OECD reports that in the United States today, 100% of students aged six-sixteen are required to attend school, but the graduation rate (completion rate) of those who are able to successfully navigate just a few more years of that system drops down to below 85%.

In the United States today, we are well aware of the teacher shortage that exists in every state, in virtually every school district. Classrooms across America are vacant or staffed by long-term substitutes.

The reason we have a shortage is not because little boys and girls no longer dream of being teachers. The reason we have a shortage is because once teachers enter into the profession, more than ever before, they are deciding that there is no way they can do the difficult work required of them for thirty or more years. They sign up to do the job, enter their classrooms, and within only a few years, the vast majority have decided to move on. They are not supported. They are not groomed. They are not grown.

Many of us are familiar with the writings of Malcolm Gladwell where he describes the need to practice a task for 10,000 hours before becoming a master. To a teacher who works 40 hours a week, 40 weeks a year, this means he/she would have to practice being a teacher for a minimum of 6.25 years to develop a sense of mastery. Mastery of the position as it is today, not even taking into account the evolution of the job and its constant revision of "best" practices. The average new teacher today lasts less than five years before moving on, well before becoming a master.

In states across America today, to tackle the teacher shortage, decisions are made that at first glance appear to be solutions, but, in reality, simply throw more fuel on the fire. States have decided to allow teachers to work without a license and designated training, in some cases for up to three years. Administrators are given the green light to remove or non-renew any teacher who is not performing in their first few years. This self-fulfilling cycle of hire, replace, hire, replace, gets perpetuated as administrators focus their attention, not on supporting the new who need it the most, but on the veterans who fall outside of the cycle. After all, in many administrators' minds, if a new teacher is not performing at a mastery level, they can just be replaced by someone new. There is no need to train, coach, or support, when you can just scrap and start over again. In schools of poverty this is even more apparent and prevalent.

In many states, the path to certification has less to do with learning the art of instruction and the nuances of pedagogy and more to do with the ability to pass a content-specific exam. These newly certified teachers walk into their classrooms filled with academic knowledge, but get frustrated when they are unable to translate that knowledge into learning for their students.

We have states who have responded to national accountability legislation by enacting strict evaluation policies. These policies have teachers who were once willing to ask for help and support from their superiors and peers, now afraid to show vulnerability and express any professional development needs, for fear of those insecurities being used against them. In our quest to hold schools accountable, we have perpetuated the crisis by creating teachers who have stagnated in their growth, administrators who have an inability to successfully support and train, and new teachers filling the growing number of vacancies in every school across the country.

Right now we are seeing the struggles with the inability to retain quality teachers. Soon we will begin to see the inability to find quality leaders as the pool of experts and masters decreases. Fewer quality leaders will exponentially heighten the critical nature of the epidemic.

If we want to address the epidemic we are currently facing, sure money would go a long way, but the real issue is not the lack of a pipeline; the issue is the lack of support once inside. We have to allow for a system of growth, a system of improvement, a system of individuals.

In elementary schools today, we understand the importance of early literacy intervention. We know that students should be given tremendous support in their first four years of school to gain foundational skills that will set them up for future success. It is time that we begin to model this same expectation with the teachers we employ. We have to provide intensive support early on. The only way to become great at anything is through repeated practice, repeated struggles, repeated feedback, and repeated support.

Let's work to eliminate the teacher shortage by doing what matters most. Let's support the teachers we have. Let's remove the labels we place on their abilities. Let's focus on growth over achievement and begin to understand that what we say is best practice for our students is often best practice for our teachers too.

Our future depends on it.

YOU CAN HAVE CONTROL OR YOU CAN HAVE GROWTH, BUT YOU CAN'T HAVE BOTH.

~

Why does it all matter?

A Penny for My Thoughts:

Why does it all matter?

A Penny for Their Thoughts:

Conclusion

We believe there are no taboo topics in education. In classrooms and schools everywhere, educators do the work that prepares students for their futures. We spend our days helping our students explore and discover and evolve. Yet, we have a tendency to avoid the very ideas that would aid us in our own evolution. We shy away from the discussions that will improve the work we do, instead of actively engaging in them. This is not something we can continue to do. Our work is too important. It matters too much. Allowing ourselves to remain silent cannot, and should not, be an option. But knowing where to start can feel impossible.

When we set out to write this book, it began as an idea to start conversations. Dave and I, though our experiences are varied, share the opinion that in order to grow, we have to be willing to push the boundaries and challenge those around us. That it is necessary to have any conversation, *especially* the hard ones. We both truly believe in the power of the individual. Because in each of us, we hold the key to effecting real, lasting change. That key is our voice.

Voice is the theme of this book, and you've hopefully encountered a variety of them. We hope our two cents provided a gateway — two voices that started the cacophony of others. Our aim in sharing our perspective was to welcome you into this space of growth, and invite you to join us in Poking the Bear. You likely disagreed with some of what we had to say; in fact, we hope you did. Because when those disagreements came about, it was our hope that you would use our words as a springboard to start your own discussions, reflections, and growth.

The conversations you have had and the reflection you have done through each chapter has likely pushed you farther outside of your comfort zone than you would normally have gone. You've likely shifted your thinking, solidified your viewpoints, and you've hopefully brought others along. Maybe you've changed the minds of others, or maybe they have changed yours. In either case, progress was made, and change happened. That is how things improve and get better. And, as we say, better is good.

We hope that you were able to debate ideas, whether they be new innovations or the status quo. Our wish is that you feel more able to challenge any belief, debate any topic, while always remembering to separate the idea from the person.

Letting sleeping bears lie, if you will, is how we end up with stagnant and ineffective practices that no longer serve us or others. Allowing things to remain as they are, without question, is the destruction of progress. When faced with the idea that people will be uncomfortable with your voice, it is our hope that those who know you well will see your words for what they are. A truth spoken not out of rudeness or malice, but out of love and a desire for a brighter future. A voice that is so consumed with passion about something that it just could not stay silent. A person who believes in what they are saying and must put it out into the world to be heard.

But let us always remember that our voices are not the only ones. We should never be so arrogant as to believe our passion or opinion is the only one to be heard. We are only as smart as those who surround us and only as knowledgeable as those we listen to. We strive to start conversations, not only so our own voices can be heard, but so that we can hear others. We wish to have our ideas questioned and our beliefs challenged because we may be wrong! It is when we cling to our own ideas and repeat them consistently that the trouble begins, so we must always be open to the opposing viewpoint.

At this point, you have hopefully begun to see the value that comes when you Poke the Bear. You have started to witness the power your voice holds, if you are willing to engage in challenging conversation. You have empowered yourself and others to take on the most difficult questions of our profession, and presumably begun to ask more questions of your own. As you reach the end of this book, we can only hope that your journey has just begun. Take this new perspective, this spark, and fan the flames. Call others into this mission of continued evolution. Continue pushing the boundaries and opening the door to new learning.

Use your power to make a difference. Use your voice to poke the bear.

Bibliography

Annie E. Casey Foundation. (2021). *Children in title I schools by Race and ethnicity: Kids Count Data Center.* KIDS COUNT Data Center. Retrieved November 13, 2021, from https://datacenter.kidscount.org.

Anser, M.K., Yousaf, Z., Nassani, A.A. *et al.* Dynamic linkages between poverty, inequality, crime, and social expenditures in a panel of 16 countries: two-step GMM estimates. *Economic Structures* 9, 43 (2020). https://doi.org/10.1186/s40008-020-00220-6

Banerjee, A.V. & Duflo, E. (2011). *Poor economics: A radical rethinking of the way to fight global poverty.* New York: Public Affairs.

Chardin, M., & Novak, K. R. (2020). *Equity by design: Delivering on the power and promise of UDL* (1st ed.). Corwin.

Ciolan, L. E. (2013). Play to learn, learn to play: creating better opportunities for learning in early childhood. *Procedia - Social and Behavioral Sciences, 76*, 186–189. https://doi.org/10.1016/j.sbspro.2013.04.096

Danielson, C. (2021). *Enhancing Professional Practice: A Framework for Teaching (Professional Development)* (2nd ed.). Association for Supervision & Curriculum Development.

Dintersmith, T. (2019). *What School Could Be: Insights and Inspiration from Teachers Across America* (Illustrated ed.). Edu21C Foundation.

241

Engle, P. and Black, M. (2008). *The Effect of Poverty on Child Development andEducational Outcomes.* Annals of New York Academy of Science. 243-256.

Fullan, M. (2001) *Leading in a Culture of Change.* Jossey-Bass.

Garet, M. S., Porter, A. C., Desimone, L., Birman, B. F., & Yoon, K. S. (2001). What Makes Professional Development Effective? Results From a National Sample of Teachers. *American Educational Research Journal, 38*(4), 915–945. https://doi.org/10. 3102/00028312038004915.

Hattie, J.A.C. (2003, October). Teachers make a difference: What is the research evidence? Paper presented at the Building Teacher Quality: What does the research tell us ACER Research Conference, Melbourne, Australia. Retrieved from http://research.acer.edu.au/research_conference_2003/4/

Loewus, L. (2021, June 4). *Why teachers leave-or don't: A look at the numbers.* Education Week. Retrieved October 15, 2021, fromhttps://www.edweek.org/teaching-learning/why-teachers-leave-or-dont-a-look-at-the-numbers/2021/05.

Minor, C. (2018). *We Got This.: Equity, Access, and the Quest to Be Who Our Students Need Us to Be* (Illustrated ed.). Heinemann.

National Center for Educational Statistics, U.S. Department of Education. (2019). Characteristics of public school teachers. In *Digest of Education Statistics 2019.* Retrieved November 13, 2021 from https://nces.ed.gov/programs/coe/indicator/clr.

National Center for Educational Statistics, U.S. Department of Education. (2019). Characteristics of public school principals. In *Digest of Education Statistics 2019.* Retrieved November 13, 2021 from https://nces.ed.gov/programs/coe/indicator/cls.

National Student Council. (2018, June). *National Student Council-Raising Student Voice and Participation Executive Summary*. NASSP. https://www.natstuco.org/wp-content/uploads/2018/06/NASSPFY18-0016_RSVP-ExecSummary-Brochure_F_Online.pdf.

National Women's Law Center (2018, April 24). *Dress coded: Black girls, bodies, and bias in D.C. schools*. National Women's Law Center Resource. https://nwlc.org/resources/dresscoded/.

OECD (2016), *PISA 2015 Results (Volume I): Excellence and Equity in Education*, PISA, OECD Publishing, Paris, https://doi.org/10.1787/9789264266490-en.

Piketty, T. (2014). *Capitalism in the twenty-first century*. (A. Goldhammer, Trans.). Cambridge Massachusetts: The Belknap Press of Harvard University Press.

Popham, J. W. (2018). *Assessment Literacy for Educators in a Hurry* (Illustrated ed.). ASCD.

Quaglia Institute for School Voice and Aspirations. (2016.) School voice report 2016. Retrieved from Quagliainstitute.org/dms-View/School_Voice_Report_2016

Ryan, R. M., & Deci, E. L. (2000). Self-determination theory and the facilitation of intrinsic motivation, social development, and well-being. American Psychologist, 55, 68-78.

Spiro, J. (2010). *Leading Change Step-by-Step: Tactics, Tools, and Tales* (1sted.). Jossey-Bass.

Stiglitz, J.E. (2019). *People, power, and profits: Progressive capitalism for an age of discontent*. New York: W. W. Norton & Company, Ltd.

Wagner, T., & Dintersmith, T. (2016). *Most likely to succeed: Preparing our kids for the innovation era*. Scribner.

Wormeli, R. (2018). *Fair Isn't Always Equal, 2nd edition: Assessment &* *Grading in the Differentiated Classroom* (second edition). Stenhouse Publishers.

About the Authors

Katelynn:

Katelynn is a middle school Language Arts and Social Studies educator in the suburbs of Chicago. She is a dynamic educator who is passionate about student voice and empowerment, promoting equity, and valuing teachers as professionals. It is her belief that what we teach goes far beyond our content—we are teaching our students to become active members of their society who have a positive impact on the world.

Katelynn has presented at various state and national conferences on assessment & grading practices, language arts instruction, social emotional learning, and equitable teaching practices. She has contributed chapters to innovative books on educational practice, including *The New Teacher's Guide to Overcoming Common Challenges* and *100 No-Nonsense Things that ALL Teachers Should STOP Doing.* You can connect with her on social media @kngiordano. When she's not out working to change the educational system, she spends time with her husband and her cat, and can usually be found reading a book.

Dave:

As an educator for more than two decades, Dave has earned a reputation for being a disruptor of the status quo, an innovator, and a change agent. Having served as a classroom teacher, school-based administrator, central office director, and professor of Educational Leadership, he often uses real-life stories and examples of his own life and career to describe why and how we need to confront "the way we have always done it." He speaks, consults, and partners with districts around the country and loves to keep learning and growing.

Dave is a father of four, living life in the panhandle of Florida. He has written multiple books, including *Omniscient, It's Like Riding a Bike: How to make learning last a lifetime,* *Bold Humility*, and *Making Assessment Work for Educators Who Hate Data but Love Kids.*

You can contact him via social media : @daveschmittou or you can join the thousands of others who connect with him via his cell phone 734-377-3457.

PUBLISHING